Baby-Led Weaning:

Fresh and Easy Recipe Book

What, When, & How Much To Feed Your Baby

Layla Stephens

Book Description

Encourage your little one to become an independent feeder!

Are you thinking about introducing your little one to solid foods? Do you want to know about the foods your little one can eat? Have you been hearing of baby-led weaning but don't know what it is about? Do you have any concerns about baby-led weaning? Do you want to learn more about it? Are you wondering about how to prepare your baby's food? If you answered yes to one or more of these questions, this is the perfect book for you!

Baby-led weaning has become quite a buzzword in parenting circles, and for all the right reasons! This feeding approach is simply known as "BLW." It refers to a style of feeding where babies feed themselves. Taking care of a baby is a full-time responsibility. During the initial six months or so, their primary source of sustenance is formula, breast milk, or a combination of the two. If you are thinking about introducing solid foods to your baby after that time, but aren't sure how to go about it, BLW offers a refreshing approach.

BLW is not only easy and convenient, it allows you to bond with your little one, too! It also encourages them to start feeding themselves from the get-go, improves their motor skills, reduces the chances of picky eating behavior, and is better than pre-packaged or processed baby foods. What more? The entire family can start eating together once your baby learns to feed themselves! In this book, you will be introduced to a variety of recipes that are ideal for BLW and are incredibly simple to prepare.

In this book, you will learn about:

- the meaning of baby-led weaning (BLW) and the benefits that offers
- signs your baby is ready for BLW
- foods ideal for BLW
- what to watch out for during BLW
- how to prepare food for BLW
- a simple checklist to get started
- sample feeding schedules for babies
- breakfast, lunch, and dinner recipes
- delicious vegan and vegetarian recipes for BLW, and much more!

So what are you waiting for? Are you excited to get your little one started on solid foods the healthy way? If yes, this book will act as your guide every step of the way!

CONTENTS

Breakfast Recipes

Lunch Recipes

Vegetarian Dinner Recipes

Vegan Dinner Recipes

Meat Dinner Recipes

Snacks

Savory Frozen Recipes

Sweet Frozen Recipes

Introduction

"There are places in the heart you don't even know exist until you love a child."
Anne Lamott

Welcoming a baby home and stepping into parenthood are unforgettable milestones. One such milestone in transitioning your baby to solid foods. If you are reading this book, your baby is probably close to the age of eating solid foods. This is one transition most parents eagerly await. If you have been hearing about baby-led weaning, want to learn more about it, or have just started your research, this book has all the answers you are looking for. Also, kudos to you for wanting to try baby-led weaning.

Baby-led weaning, or "BLW," is a simple feeding style where the baby is encouraged to feed on its own from the beginning. This actually is as simple as it sounds. Perhaps the most attractive benefit of BLW is that the baby starts eating what you eat. Also, it helps to develop their motor skills, reduces the chances of picky eating behaviors, and makes it easier for parents to introduce a variety of foods to their tiny tots.

Despite all the benefits it offers, you might have some concerns about introducing solids to your baby. Maybe you are worried about allergic reactions, or even worse, the thought of your baby choking on food. Well, it is time to put all these (understandable) fears to rest. With a little conscious effort, vigilance, and patience, your baby will start eating on their own without issue.

Are you wondering how I know all this? I think it's time for an introduction. Hello, my name is Layla Stephens. I am a 26-year-old mother to three wonderful children. I used to be a midwife before turning into a full-time happy and proud homemaker. I am incredibly passionate about healthy cooking and eating, fitness, and reading. I know how wonderful parenthood can be, but I also know the struggles that come with it. Whether it is getting your baby used to a routine, or their feeding schedule, there are a lot of aspects involved. One such aspect is feeding your little one. When my babies were around six months old I decided to try BLW. Let me tell you, it changed my life! It not only made it easier to feed my babies, it reduced most of the fuss associated with mealtimes, too. Also, I noticed my babies were happier when they were eating by themselves.

That said, I also know the struggles associated with it. From worries about whether you are choosing the right foods, to the concern of gagging and choking, I went through it all. I was worried whether my little ones were eating enough, and if their little bodies were getting the nourishment they needed. Simply put, it was a rollercoaster ride. I tried different foods, recipes, and preparations. Once I started sharing my suggestions with other mothers and got positive feedback, I wanted to do more. This ignited the spark in my mind and heart to compile all the advice I have on this topic in one place. This, coupled with my personal experience, the days I spent researching, and my passion for nutrition and fitness, further strengthened my resolve. Dear parents, I have got your back! I will help you every step of the way as you introduce solid foods to your little bundle of joy. Any apprehensions you have about BLW will go away once you go through the information given in this book. By using the tips and simple suggestions in this book, you can rest easy knowing that your baby is getting all the nourishment they need. From learning about foods that are ideal for BLW, to preparation styles, to foods to avoid, you will find all the information you need here, in one place.

Also, I have compiled numerous recipes that will make BLW easier for you. These recipes are divided into different categories for your convenience: breakfast, lunch, dinner, and snacks. The best part is, these recipes are tried, tested, and baby-approved. And, if you or your family have dietary restrictions, no problem; I have ensured there is a good mix of vegetarian, vegan, and meat-based recipes that will leave your baby wanting more.

(Don't forget to use the food reaction chart and the allergy swap information given in this book to keep a track of your baby's likes and dislikes. Once you are armed with all of this information, getting started with BLW will become easier than you thought. So, are you eager to learn more about all this? If yes, let's get started!)

Your Free Gift!

As a way of saying thanks for your purchase, I'm offering the BLW Shopping Guide for FREE to my readers.
To get instant access just click on the title below:

LaylaStephens.com/BLWFreeGift

Inside the guide, you will discover:

- The best most affordable products I have tried & tested
- A full checklist of what you need to get started
- Bonus baby related must have products

If you want to save hours of research and money spent, I have simplified it all for you, so make sure to grab the free book.

Understanding Baby-Led Weaning

The mantra of baby-led weaning is, "no baby food, no feeding, and no spoons." To a parent, all this probably sounds too good to be true. Well, prepare yourself to be pleasantly surprised! A common worry most parents have, especially if their baby is close to the age where they can start introducing solid foods, is how to go about introducing this change in feeding to their baby. It is a significant milestone. So, do not forget to celebrate it! However, this developmental milestone can become a source of stress and anxiety for some parents when they don't know what to give their little one. Sure, your pediatrician can give you a list of recommended solid foods; that said, how do you get your baby used to eating these solid foods? There are two methods: the first one is a conventional method, where foods are pureed and then spoon-fed to babies. The second method is more interactive–baby-led weaning.

The traditional method has been around for decades, and this is how most babies were weaned. It is slightly problematic, because it doesn't give the baby any control over their mealtime, like with how much food they eat. Also, the baby does not get to learn how to use their hands to feed themselves. There is no scope for self-regulation whatsoever. These are some of the reasons BLW, as an alternative method, has been getting so much traction lately.

What Does BLW Mean?

The concept of BLW is quite simple. Even though it was introduced only about 15 years ago, it has become incredibly popular; and for all the right reasons. For the first few months of their lives, babies have breast milk, formula, or a combination of both. The process of weaning is essentially introducing your little one to solid foods. BLW promotes the introduction of solid foods to your little one through self-feeding. The ideal time to start is when your baby is around six months old. Unlike the traditional spoon-feeding method of purees, mostly popular in Western countries, in BLW the baby is in charge. Usually, babies go from a liquid diet to eating purees that are fed by their parents, to family foods as they grow older. However, with BLW, babies are offered baby-sized foods from the get-go. Instead of taking a spoon and trying to feed your baby what they don't want to eat, you simply need to give them a plate of food (specially prepared for BLW purposes) and let them eat by themselves. Around this age, babies are capable of grasping and can develop their motor skills through BLW.

Benefits BLW Offers

A baby is crying loudly, and fat tears are rolling down their cheeks. A haggard-looking parent is trying to feed the crying infant some form of puree. Regardless of how hard the parent tries, the baby does not want to eat it, and the battle of wills thus continues. This is a scene most parents have experienced. Now, imagine this situation. The baby is given finger-sized food that they are very happily holding in their hands and eating at their own pace. If the first situation fills you with dread and the second with happiness, what do you think is the right path? The best way to introduce solid foods to your little one is through BLW. After going through all the advantages it offers, you will want to get started immediately.

It's Easy

It is incredibly easy. You don't have to worry about holding any utensils, forcefully feeding your little one, or getting into any battle of wills. Instead, the baby is in charge, and they determine when they want to eat, how much they want to eat, and when to stop. It is also easy because your baby enjoys what they are eating, and this by itself is quite rewarding to see.

Healthy Eating Habits

 BLW is believed to promote healthy eating habits and behaviors later in life. (Magda Sachs, 2011). When compared to those weaned using the traditional weaning style of puree feeding, BLW babies were more aware of their hunger and fullness cues. (A. Brown and M. D. Lee, 2015).

Reduces Picky Eating

You might have seen children who refuse to eat certain food, or babies who are extremely picky. Well, if you want to raise a child who eats everything, BLW is the way to go. One fear most parents have about feeding their babies is, "will they like it?" The chances of picky eating are reduced to a great extent with BLW. (Sonya L Cameron et al., 2012).

Nutritious and Affordable

When compared to baby food, especially the pre-packaged and processed variants, BLW is extremely affordable and more nutritious. Making food at home is not only cheaper, it gives you complete control over the quality of ingredients used, and the quantities used in the recipe.

Motor Skills

With BLW, babies are encouraged to feed themselves. If they are just learning how to grasp things, this feeding style will give them more control over how to use their arms. In a way, it helps develop their motor skills and encourages them to understand how they are supposed to pick up food items and put them in their mouth. Initially, there will be quite a mess, but soon your baby will learn how to eat properly.

Family Time

Your baby will also become a part of family mealtime. Forget about feeding your little one before feeding yourself. From now on, the entire family can sit together and eat. Even if it is slightly messy, this is family time, and nothing can replace it.

How to Know if Your Baby is Ready for BLW

Now comes the big question: how do you know if your baby is ready to start eating solid foods? Usually, it is recommended that you need to wait until they are about six months old before you can introduce solids in any form. Apart from this, you should also start looking out for different signs that will help determine whether your baby is ready to start consuming solids or not. This is a decision that you should make only after considering the advice given by your child's primary healthcare provider or pediatrician.

Here are some simple signs that clearly indicate when your baby is ready to start eating solid foods other than their regular feeds of breast milk or formula.

   • Your baby can sit up by themselves and can hold their head up without any support.
   • They are showing interest in the foods that you eat. Whether it is watching you intently as you eat, or trying to reach for the food you eat, this shows eagerness and interest.
   • Developmentally, they are at an age where they can comfortably move the food around in their mouth and have lost the tongue-thrust reflex. (This means that your baby does not spit the food out automatically when you put it in their mouth.)
   • They are showing an eagerness to start participating in mealtime. They do this by smacking their lips or trying to reach for food.

When you start paying attention to their body language, you will know when your baby wants to start eating solid foods. Babies are biologically programmed to want to eat what their parents are eating. This is because if they see you eat it, it means it's safe for consumption.

Chapter

02

How To Prepare Food?

Babies are tiny humans, of course, but their digestive systems are still in the developing phase, and aren't exactly the same as ours yet. They are also learning to improve their motor skills at this stage. Now, when it comes to BLW, they don't yet have the coordination needed to feed themselves as easily as adults can. So, the food you present needs to be easy for them to pick up and eat. In this chapter, you will learn about a variety of foods that you can add to your baby's diet, and ones that you must avoid at all costs. By using the simple suggestions given here, BLW will become easier for you and baby alike.

Foods to Include

Other than the foods discussed in the section "Foods to Avoid," you can give your baby everything else. That said, be mindful of the spices and flavorings used. The good news is you don't have to spend any time looking for recipes online. All the information you need is given in the subsequent chapters.

The most common foods that are recommended for starting BLW are:

- Sweet potatoes
- Apples
- Bananas
- Broccoli florets
- Cantaloupes and other melons
- Proteins such as beef, tofu, and chicken
- Cooked eggs
- Breads
- Avocados

Ideas to Prepare Food

How the food is prepared is crucial when it comes to BLW. The preparation also depends upon whether your baby has a palmar or pincer grasp. A palmar grip is when the baby brings all of their fingers inward toward the palm to hold anything. They usually use this until they are about eight or nine months old. After this, they develop a pincer grasp. This refers to their ability to pick up objects using their thumb and index finger.

If your baby is using a palmar grip, give them finger-shaped food. The ingredients must be cut into fingers that are about three inches long and half an inch wide. It makes it easy for them to grasp the food served. If they are using a pincer grasp, usually after they are about nine months old, you can give them chunks of soft and easily mashed food that can be eaten with or without a spoon.

Even after your baby has developed a pincer grasp, keep giving them bigger pieces of tender foods, such as wedges of avocado, or even an omelet. As your baby grows, you can slowly start introducing them to smaller-sized foods.

The foods presented should be such that they are easy for the baby to pick up. They cannot pick up small pieces of food until they are at least nine months old. So, giving your six month old boiled chickpeas is not only a choking hazard, they won't know how to eat it, either.

Similarly, ensure the foods you offer aren't too slippery. If your baby cannot grip them in their hand, they cannot eat them. For instance, leave a little peel on fresh fruits such as kiwis, bananas, mangoes, and avocados while serving.

Avoid cutting foods into circles, and do not give them round-shaped foods. It means you shouldn't give them discs of carrots or cucumbers. Such foods can easily become a choking hazard for the baby. Instead, cut them into the shape of fingers or wedges.

You can also give your little one pureed foods. Yes, even with BLW, you can give your baby purees. Depending on whether they can hold the spoon or not, encourage your little one to try them. You will need to pre-load the spoon and hand it over to your little one. Or, if you don't mind a little mess, let your baby scoop it up into their hand and feed themselves.

Foods to Avoid

The idea of introducing new foods to your baby can be quite exciting. You might want them to taste everything you eat. That said, their body is still developing, and it's not yet ready to eat everything that adults can. Certain foods can become choking hazards, while others are unsuited for babies because of their underdeveloped digestive and immune systems. Here is a list of foods that should be avoided until your baby is at least 12 months old. If you are adding any of these foods, ensure that your pediatrician has given you the go-ahead.

Honey

One food that should be avoided until your baby is at least 12 months old is honey. Though it is natural and delicious, the spores of a specific bacteria present in it can trigger botulism.

Cow's Milk

Babies who are under 12 months old should not be given cow's milk, because it is hard for them to digest. It also doesn't offer the nutrients babies need for their growth and development. Further, cow's milk is one of the most common sources of food allergies (Rosie Vincent et al., 2021). Ideally, avoiding cow's milk is a good idea.

Certain Types of Fish

Certain types of fish have high levels of mercury, and it can prove extremely dangerous for babies. Some common types of fish that you need to stay away from are: fresh tuna, swordfish, shark, and king mackerel as per the guidelines released by FDA about mercury content in fish in 2012. Raw shellfish or any lightly-cooked shellfish such as oysters, clams, or mussels must be avoided too. These foods increase the risk of food poisoning.

Cured and Smoked Meats

Smoked and cured meats contain nitrates and a variety of chemicals that are harmful to your baby. They are also rich in sodium, and unhealthy animal fats do not do your baby's health any favors.

Refined Flour

Refined flour is mostly found in different types of processed and pre-packaged treats. Refined flour and foods made with it should be avoided because it's one of the most common irritants to the digestive system. (Antonella Cianferoni, 2016). It can cause food intolerances. Even if you are making waffles or pancakes at home, opt for whole-grain flour or whole meal instead of the processed variants.

Salt

Salt is harmful to a baby's kidneys. It can also increase the risk of cardiovascular disorders later in life. (Nikki E Emmerik et al., 2020). At least until your baby is 12 months old, avoid adding salt to their food, or even to their cooking water. Don't use stock or gravy cubes, and avoid salty foods such as: chips, bacon, deli meats, crackers, and ready-to-eat meals.

Saturated Fats

Ensure you avoid giving your baby saturated fats as much as you possibly can. Most pre-packaged, processed, and sugary foods are high in saturated fats. While selecting packed foods ensure to carefully read through the nutrition labels.

Sugar

Sugar must not be a part of your infant's diet until they are at least 12 months old. This can disrupt their appetite. Babies usually have a natural affinity for anything sweet, but giving them sugary treats, especially ones made with processed ingredients is a bad idea. Instead, encourage them to have naturally sweet foods such as fruits. As a rule of thumb, avoid all processed and pre-packaged foods, and give your baby natural or homemade foods.

Whole Nuts

Whole nuts and peanuts are choking hazards. Ground peanuts or peanut butter can be given to babies. However, if you have a family history of nut allergies, or any other food allergies, consult your family doctor before adding these foods to your baby's diet.

Raw Eggs

Eggs are healthy, to be sure, but ensure your baby doesn't eat raw eggs. Gulping down raw eggs can trigger digestive distress and skin irritation.

Certain Types of Cheese

Pasteurized full-fat cheeses including cottage cheese, mild cheddar, and cream cheese can be given to babies who are over six months old. Please do not give them mold-ripened soft cheeses such as roquefort, camembert, or brie, because they are made with unpasteurized milk and increase the risk of contracting listeria.

Rice Drinks

Children under the age of five years must not be given any rice drinks to substitute breast milk or formula. They shouldn't even be given cow's milk until they are at least a year old. When compared to other grains, rice absorbs arsenic quite easily. Rice is permissible because stringent protocols are set in place by different national governments to regulate the quality of rice reaching the markets. For instance, the USDA (United States Department of Agriculture) is responsible for ensuring this in the US. So, it is predominantly a safety measure to ensure your baby doesn't consume rice drinks. Even if you are using rice milk as a substitute, shifting to any other form of milk, like cashew or almond, is a better idea.

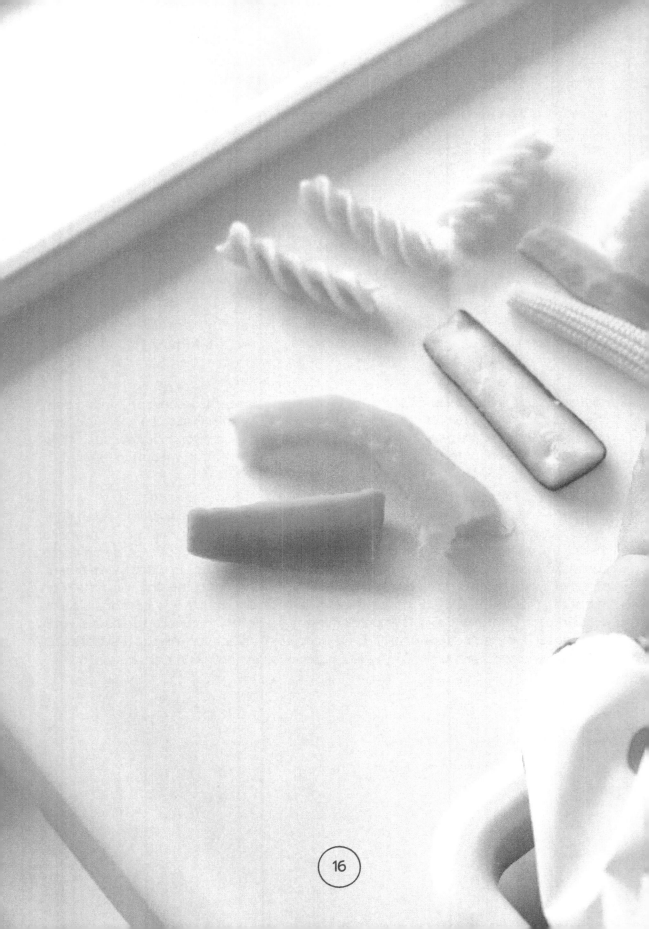

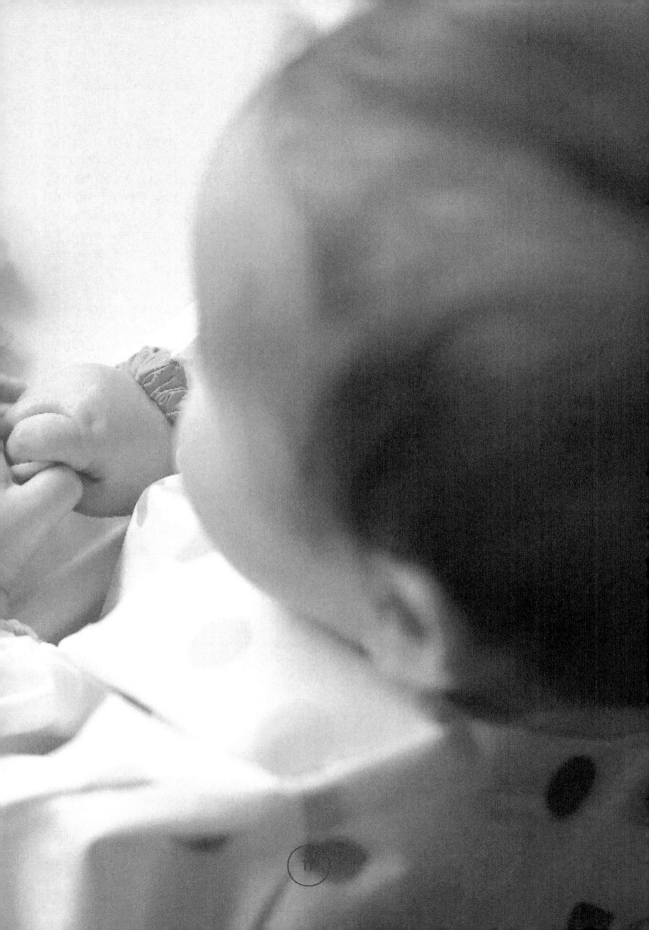

Gagging and Choking

Gagging and choking might sound the same, but they are not. Even though they are used synonymously, they are extremely different.

Gagging is quite common in babies when they are six or seven months old. This depends mostly on the texture of the food that is given to them. Learning to eat finger foods might sound extremely simple to an adult, but it's a completely new experience for a baby. They need to learn how to chew, swallow, and breathe simultaneously. If your baby is gagging, you don't have to panic because it is normal and it essentially means they swallowed something they haven't chewed yet and their body is preventing it from going further down. Gagging is a helpful mechanism that reduces the risk of choking.

Gagging is usually quite noisy, and it's a built-in safety mechanism we all have. It usually occurs when trying to bring up food that is not yet swallowed. It's more like a process of coughing until the food is brought up. The gag reflex is quite strong initially, and it slowly shifts further back in the mouth. Gagging is your body's natural reaction to prevent choking. As the baby ages, their gag reflex reduces. This means, they can swallow food without any difficulty. The gag reflex starts easing at around the same time they can start eating solid foods. The gag reflex of a nine-month-old baby is almost the same as that of an adult.

Choking, on the other hand, is quite serious, and should not be ignored. While gagging is loud and noisy, choking is silent. It occurs when a large piece of food, or any other foreign particle, is lodged in the airway. It essentially blocks the airway and causes extreme distress to the baby. Babies can turn blue or even grab at their throat because they are unable to breathe.

Worrying about gagging or choking is quite common in parents who are introducing solids to their babies, especially for the first time. The simplest way to avoid choking is to learn about foods that are choking hazards. Even finger foods need to be prepared safely and appropriately and cut in a size that is ideal for the baby to chew on.

The chances of choking during BLW are incredibly low. That said, preparing yourself for all situations is needed. This might be something you don't even want to think about, but learning what's to be done in case of a choking emergency makes all the difference.

What to Do if Your Baby is Choking

If your baby is choking, ensure that you stay calm and do not panic.

• Notice whether your baby's cough is forceful or if they are crying quite hard. Do not administer first aid if you notice either. Both of these things are a sign that their airway is not fully blocked and they are coughing or crying to push it out.

• Administer first aid and call 911 immediately if you notice your baby's skin takes on a bluish tinge or if they are struggling to breathe.

• If your baby is unconscious and you notice the object that's blocking their airway, try to physically remove it with your finger.

When it comes to BLW, ensure that you are always around when your baby is eating. Your baby shouldn't be left unsupervised while they are eating. This is not only a precautionary measure, it also gives you a chance to see how they are eating. Whether it is a puree or any soft foods, please don't leave them unsupervised. Also, make sure your baby is comfortable while seated. They need to sit upright and shouldn't be distracted while eating. These simple practices will reduce the risk of choking. Apart from all of this, please be incredibly patient and prepare yourself to deal with the invariable mess associated with this process.

Common Choking Hazards

•   Whole grapes
•   Hard candies
•   Popcorn
•   Peaches, plums, cherries, and other fruits with stones (they are safe once the seed is removed)
•   Hard nuts such as: hazelnuts, macadamia nuts, pecans, cashews, brazil nuts, and almonds
•   Extra dry or crusty bread
•   Extremely moist bread
•   Hard and coin-shaped foods such as rounds of carrots or sausages
•   Marshmallows
•   Thick layers or spoonfuls of nut and seed butter
•   Dried fruits such as raisins, figs, and others that are slightly rounded

19

Chapter 03

Food Reactions/ Allergies

The process of introducing new food to your baby involves more steps than simply giving them something new to eat. Usually, whenever you give your baby something new, you need to wait for at least two days before trying another ingredient. This observation period is needed to ensure the food introduced is neither an allergen nor an irritant. Apart from this, paying attention to your baby's reaction to the food is important.

Food Response Tracker

Your baby might like certain foods while disliking others. Knowing their preferences gives you a chance to work on different recipes to introduce the ingredients they aren't fond of. It also makes food preparation easy when you know what they like.

The simplest way to do this is by maintaining a food reaction chart. In this chart, you must note:

- the ingredient you introduced;
- the form in which it was given;
- when it was given; and,
- your little one's reaction.

Here is a sample of how a typical food reaction chart looks:

Ingredient Introduced	Form in Which it Was Served	Like/Dislike	Date and Time
Avocado	Wedges	Like	05/02/2022

Allergy Swap

In the previous chapter, you were introduced to some foods that are unfit for babies. Some foods are a choking hazard, while others can trigger allergies. Understand that a food allergy is not the same as a sensitivity or intolerance. Sensitivity refers to a condition where the body cannot digest certain ingredients and results in gastric distress. On the other hand, an allergic reaction can be serious because of the immune response involved in this process. A food allergy increases the risk of anaphylaxis, a life-threatening allergic reaction that closes the airway. This is why you must always introduce only a single ingredient at a time and wait for a few days before introducing another.

Here is a simple chart you can use to keep a track of any allergic response or sensitivity noticed after introducing an ingredient:

Food	Date and Time	Any Reaction of Symptom You Noticed	The Duration Within Which The Symptoms Started Appearing	Quantity of the food given	Does the reaction occur whenever the said ingredient is given?	Duration of the reaction	Your response to it and did it help?
Porridge made with wheat	5th Feb, 2022	Slight bloating and gas	Within 30 mins	3 tbsp	Yes	Few hours	Substituted wheat with rice

Allergic reactions can range from mild, to moderate, to severe. It can range from hives, coughing, and digestive troubles, to difficulty breathing, severe swelling of the lips, tongue, and throat, and loss of consciousness. Ideally, avoiding the foods discussed in the previous chapter until your baby is at least 12 months old is a good idea.

In this section, let's look at some common foods and their substitutes to reduce the chances of any allergies or sensitivities.

• Peanut butter or any other nut-based butter can be replaced with sunflower seed butter or sesame paste.
• Eggs can be substituted with ground a chia seed and water mixture, a flaxseed and water mixture, or a mixture of water, oil, and baking powder.
• Cow's milk can be substituted with soy or pea milk.
• Soybeans can be replaced with lentils or beans.
• Fish can be replaced with meat, poultry, chia, flaxseeds, or even hemp hearts.
• Meat can be replaced with nut butter, beans, tofu, poultry, or legumes.
• Wheat can be substituted with corn, oats, quinoa, buckwheat, or other whole grains.

When it comes to your baby, do not ignore your gut. If you feel nervous giving your baby certain foods, or notice they gag more while eating certain things, avoid them. You can revisit such foods later. As your baby's self-feeding skills improve, you can start introducing more foods.

Chapter 04

Checklist to Get Started

By now, you must be incredibly excited and eager to get your little one started with BLW. As exciting as it might sound, there are some essentials you will need. After all, can you paint without the required painting supplies? Similarly, you need a few essential items to ensure the entire process goes on smoothly and with as few bumps as possible.

Overview of the Checklist

- Blender or food processor
- Vegetable steamer
- Ice cube trays
- Plastic wrap
- Ziplock bags
- High chair
- Cushion
- Splash mat
- Bibs
- Face cloths
- Silicone placemat
- Bowls
- Cups
- Sippy cup
- Plates

Now, let's see how some of these items will come in handy.

High Chair

Your baby will need a dedicated seat that is meant only for eating. This is where the high chair comes into the picture. These days, a variety of high chair models are available to choose from and they are quite affordable. They are all easy to assemble and can be taken anywhere required. While you select a high chair, the only condition you must remember is to opt for one that is easy to clean.

Cushion

Your baby will spend quite some time in this high chair. So, get them a cushion to sit on. Whatever you opt for, make it a point that it is easy to clean.

Splash Mat

In BLW, the baby will be encouraged to feed on their own, which essentially means there will be quite a mess. Your baby's motor skills are still developing, and this means they will drop a lot of food. At times, the room might look like a battleground with food splattered across all possible surfaces. To avoid such situations, you need a splash mat. Place this mat on the floor and keep the high chair on it. These mats are not only easy to clean, they ensure you don't have to spend a lot of time on your hands and knees cleaning the floor.

Bib

It's not just the floor and other surfaces you need to worry about. With BLW, the integrity of your baby's clothes is also compromised. If you don't want to be constantly washing your baby's clothes, purchase a couple of bibs at least. Instead of a regular bib that's tied around the neck, opt for long-sleeved coverall bibs. These bibs usually have a tieback and can be easily put on and removed as well. They also cover most of your baby's body, so the cleaning up of them afterwards becomes more manageable.

Dishes and Utensils

Do you have different sets of dinnerware at home? Perhaps one set is for daily use and the other for special occasions. You might also have specific cutlery or utensils you are fond of. Now it is time to get some dishes and utensils for your baby, too! After all, they can not eat off your plate, and giving them designated plates and bowls can act as a signal of mealtime.

You will need:
- a sippy cup;
- a silicone placemat;
- silicone plates; and,
- unbreakable cups, bowls, and plates.

Look for plates and bowls with multiple separators. Place them on a silicone mat to ensure they don't move as your baby starts feeding themselves.

Apart from all this, keep a couple of hand or face towels handy to make the clean up easier. Also, dear parents, please be patient during this stage! Do not lose your cool and do not get upset with your little one!

Kitchen Equipment

Making baby food at home is incredibly simple. It usually consists of cutting, blanching or boiling, blending, and steaming. These are the most commonly recommended cooking techniques.

- You can also serve them frozen foods, such as frozen apple puree popsicles! So, to make things easier, you need some basic kitchen equipment.

• You will need a blender or a food processor to make smoothies and purees.

• A vegetable steamer for steaming vegetables.

• Ice cube trays for freezing fruit pieces, smoothies, or purees that can be thawed and served.

• To ensure you are storing them properly, you will need a set of ice cube trays, plastic wrap, and Ziplock bags. For instance, you can store pureed ingredients in ice cube trays and cover them with plastic wrap before placing it in the freezer. Alternatively, you can store them in Ziplock bags too.

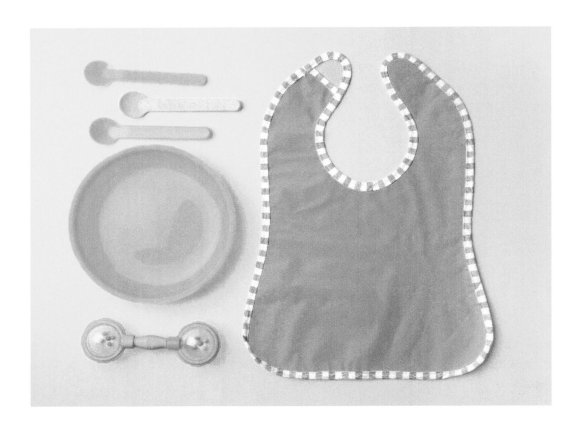

Chapter

05

BREAKFAST
RECIPES

Banana Chia Seed Pudding

Ingredients:

½ ripe banana
1 tablespoon chia seeds
6 tablespoons milk of your choice
¼ teaspoon vanilla extract (optional)

Directions:

Step 1: Chop the banana and put it in a blender.
Step 2: Pour milk into the blender. You can add any milk of your choice including breast milk.
Step 3: Add vanilla extract if using.
Step 4: Blend the mixture until you get smooth puree.
Step 5: Add chia seeds and stir the puree with a spoon. You can also give short pulses if you want to slightly powder the chia seeds.
Step 6: Pour the pudding mixture into a bowl and cover the bowl. Chill for at least 20 minutes. The chia seeds will swell up and the pudding will become thick in consistency. If your baby does not like the thick pudding, you can dilute the pudding with some more milk to suit your baby's preferred consistency.

Notes:

• You can make variations in taste by replacing banana with any other fruit that you would like to include in your baby's diet. You can add any berries or apples. You can cook the apples before adding.
• You can add a few drops of sweetener like maple syrup if desired or you could also pit a date and add it into the blender while blending, for added sweetness. You could do well without adding the sweetener when you make the pudding with banana but berries could be a bit sour, so adding a bit of sweetener can help.
• You can also make this pudding ahead of time and chill until use. It can last for about 3 days.
• Without blending the banana and chia seeds, this pudding can be enjoyed by adults as well.

 Makes: 1 baby serving
Age: 6 months +

Overnight
Blueberry Oats

Ingredients:
⅛ cup frozen blueberries
A pinch ground cinnamon
⅛ teaspoon chia seeds (optional)
¼ cup milk of your choice
3 tablespoons old fashioned oats

Directions:
Step 1: Place blueberries in a blender.
Step 2: Add milk and cinnamon. You can add any milk of your choice including breast milk.
Step 3: Add chia seeds if using.
Step 4: Blend the mixture until you get a smooth puree.
Step 5: Add oats into a bowl, if you want to serve chunky oats. Pour the blended mixture and stir well. You can also add oats into the blender along with the blended puree and give short pulses if you want to slightly grind the oats. This is advisable if you are just starting oats for the first time.
Step 6: Cover the bowl. Chill for at least 7 to 8 hours. Make sure to stir the oats before serving.

Notes:
• You can replace blueberries with any other berries or fruit of your choice.
• This breakfast recipe can be enjoyed by babies and the rest of the family as well. For adults and kids, do not blend the oats and berries.

Makes: 4 baby servings
Age: 6 months +

Strawberry Applesauce

Ingredients:

2 ½ apples, peeled and cored
1 heaping cup hulled strawberries
¼ teaspoon ground cinnamon
¼ cup water
½ teaspoon vanilla extract

Directions:

Step 1: Chop the apples and strawberries into smaller pieces.

Step 2: Put the apples into a saucepan.

Step 3: Add water into the saucepan and heat the mixture over medium-high high.

Step 4: When the mixture begins to boil, lower the heat to medium-low and cook with the lid on until the apples are slightly tender, about 12-15 minutes. Stir occasionally.

Step 5: Stir in strawberries, cinnamon, and vanilla extract. Continue cooking covered for 10-12 minutes, until the apples and strawberries are soft.

Step 6: Turn off the heat and cool for around 30 minutes.

Step 7: If you want to serve chunky sauce to your little one, mash lightly with a spoon. If you want to serve smooth sauce, blend the mixture in a blender until smooth, or the consistency you prefer.

Step 8: Pour into an airtight container and refrigerate until used. It can last for a week in the refrigerator.

Step 9: To serve: Warm the sauce and serve.

Notes:

• To freeze: Pour the blended sauce into ice cube trays. Freeze until use. It can last for three months frozen.

• You can replace strawberries with any other berry of your choice. I am sure your baby would like to try out new food every few days.

Makes: 1 baby serving
Age: 6 months +

Açai Berry
Bowl

Ingredients:

½ banana, sliced

¼ cup berries

½ packet acai puree, thawed for about 10 to 15 minutes. The acai puree should not be fully thawed, it should be semi-frozen.

½ cup milk of your choice or more if required

Chia seeds to garnish

Any other toppings of your choice

Directions:

Step 1: Place the sliced bananas on a tray and freeze until firm.

Step 2: Put the banana slices and acai puree into a blender.

Step 3: Pour the milk into the blender.

Step 4: Blend until smooth. Add more milk if required.

Step 5: Transfer into two bowls. Garnish with chia seeds and any other toppings and serve. You can serve one bowl to your baby and enjoy the other bowl yourself or give it to another kid.

Banana and Apple
Porridge

Ingredients:
½ ripe banana
½ apple, peeled and cored
1 ½ tablespoons instant oats
Water, as required

Directions:
Step 1: Peel and chop the apple and banana into small pieces.
Step 2: Place apple pieces into a small saucepan.
Step 3: Pour enough water to cover the apples.
Step 4: Place the saucepan over medium heat and cook until the apples are nice and soft.
Step 5: Turn off the heat and mash up the apples using a fork.
Step 6: While the apples are cooking, pour about ½ cup water in another saucepan. Place that saucepan over medium heat. When the water is hot, stir in the oats and cook until slightly thick. Remove the saucepan from heat.
Step 7: Stir in mashed apples and banana until well combined.
Step 8: Serve warm.

Pumpkin Pancakes

Ingredients:

½ cup cubed, cooked pumpkin or butternut squash

1 small egg (or beat a large egg and use half of it)

½ tablespoon maple syrup

2-4 drops vanilla extract

¼ cup cottage cheese or Greek-style yogurt

¼ cup rolled oats

¼ teaspoon ground cinnamon

⅛ teaspoon ground nutmeg

⅛ teaspoon ground ginger

Directions:

Step 1: Place pumpkin, egg, maple syrup, vanilla, cottage cheese (or yogurt), oats, and spices into a blender and blend until you get smooth batter.

Step 2: Pour the batter into a bowl.

Step 3: Place a non-stick pan over medium heat. When the pan is hot, pour about a tablespoonful of the batter into the pan.

Step 4: Soon bubbles will be visible on the pancake. Cook until the underside is cooked and golden brown. Turn the pancake over and cook the other side until golden brown. Take out the pancake from the pan and keep warm.

Step 5: Repeat steps 3-4 until the batter is done.

french Toast Sticks

Serves: 4 baby servings
Age: 9 months +

Ingredients:
½ small very ripe banana, sliced
3 tablespoons milk
Butter
1 large egg
4 whole-grain or sourdough bread slices, cut into fingers (about 1 inch wide)
¼ teaspoon ground cinnamon
¼ teaspoon vanilla extract
Maple syrup to serve (optional)

Directions:
Step1: Blend together banana, milk, cinnamon, vanilla extract, and egg in a blender until smooth.
Step2: Pour the mixture into a bowl. You can cook the bread sticks in a pan or in an oven. (I will give you both methods.)

For cooking in the pan:
Step 1: Place a non-stick pan with a little butter over medium heat.
Step 2: Dip the bread sticks one at a time in the egg mixture.
Step 3: Immediately lift the bread stick and place it on the pan. (You need to be quick, or else the bread will soak the mixture and will break as you lift it.)
Step 4: Place as many as can fit in the pan.
Step 5: Cook until the underside is golden brown. Turn the bread sticks over and cook the other side until golden brown.
Step 6: Remove the bread sticks from the pan and cool for a few minutes before serving.
Step 7: Cook the remaining bread sticks similarly, adding more butter to the pan as needed.

To cook in an oven:
Step 1: Line a baking sheet with parchment paper. Preheat your oven to 400°F.
Step 2: Immediately lift the bread stick and place it on the baking sheet. (You need to be quick, or else the bread will soak the mixture and will break as you lift it.)
Step 3: Bake for eight minutes, until the tops are light golden brown.
Step 4: Turn the bread sticks over and bake the other side until light golden brown.
Step 5: Serve immediately. You can serve with a little maple syrup if desired, or with applesauce, or strawberry-applesauce.

Notes:
• Store leftovers in an airtight container in the refrigerator. Use within two to three days.
• This recipe can be enjoyed by your entire family. You only need to double or triple the recipe.

Makes: 1 large baby serving
Age: 9 months +

Cottage Cheese with

Fruit

Ingredients:
½ cup full-fat cottage cheese
¼ cup chopped fruit like blueberries, strawberries, or peach (fresh or frozen)
¼ teaspoon ground cinnamon

Directions:
Step 1: Thaw the fruit if using it frozen.
Step 2: Combine cottage cheese, fruit, and cinnamon in a bowl. You can use any other fruit of your choice. You can use any one of the suggested fruits or a combination of fruits.
Step 3: Serve.

Notes:
• Store leftovers in an airtight container. It should be used within two to three days.
• You can make this recipe for babies aged 6 months +; for this, either puree the fruit or finely chop the fruit.

Makes: 6 baby servings
Age: 9 months +

Porridge Sticks
with Flavor Variations

Ingredients:
6 tablespoons milk (if making plain porridge sticks)
4 tablespoons milk (if making flavor variations)
6 tablespoons rolled oats or quick cooking oats (but not steel cut oats)

For banana porridge sticks:
½ banana, mashed

For apple porridge sticks:
⅛ cup grated apple
⅛ cup unsweetened applesauce
1 teaspoon ground cinnamon

For raspberry and coconut porridge sticks:
2 teaspoons unsweetened desiccated coconut
3 tablespoons mashed raspberries

For pumpkin porridge sticks:
⅛ cup pumpkin puree
⅛ cup grated apple
1 teaspoon pumpkin pie spice

For carrot porridge sticks:
⅛ cup grated carrot
2 tablespoons unsweetened applesauce
⅛ teaspoon ground ginger
1 teaspoon ground cinnamon
⅛ teaspoon ground nutmeg

 44

For berry porridge sticks:

¼ cup fresh or frozen blueberries, or chopped strawberries
¼ teaspoon vanilla extract

Directions:

Step 1: To make plain porridge sticks:

Step 2: Combine oats and milk in a bowl. Allow it to soak for a few minutes until it is very soft.

Step 3: Take a small, flat, microwave-safe container and spoon the oat mixture into it. Press the mixture onto the bottom of the container with the back of the spoon.

Step 4: Place the bowl in the microwave and cook on 'High' for two minutes. Check if the top of the mixture is firm. If it is not, cook for a few more seconds.

Step 5: Remove the container from the microwave and cut into sticks. Cut it while it is hot.

To make banana porridge sticks:

Step 1: Combine oats, banana, and milk in a bowl. Allow to soak for a few minutes until it is very soft.

Step 2: Take a small, flat, microwave-safe container and spoon the oat mixture into it. Press the mixture onto the bottom of the container with the back of the spoon.

Step 3: Place the bowl in the microwave and cook on 'High' for two minutes. Check if the top of the mixture is firm. If it is not, cook for a few more seconds.

Step 4: Remove the container from the microwave and cut into sticks. Cut it while it is hot.

To make apple porridge sticks:

Step 1: Combine oats, cinnamon, grated apple, applesauce, and milk in a bowl. Allow them to soak for a few minutes until very soft.

Step 2: Take a small, flat, microwave-safe container and spoon the oat mixture into it. Press the mixture onto the bottom of the container with the back of the spoon.

Step 3: Place the bowl in the microwave and cook on 'High' for two minutes. Check if the top of the mixture is firm. If it is not, cook for a few more seconds.

Step 4: Remove the container from the microwave and cut into sticks. Cut it while it is hot.

To make raspberry and coconut porridge sticks:

Step 1: Combine oats, raspberry, and milk in a bowl. Allow them to soak for a few minutes, until very soft.

Step 2: Add coconut and mix well.

Step 3: Take a small, flat, microwave-safe container and spoon the oat mixture into it. Press the mixture onto the bottom of the container with the back of the spoon.

Step 4: Place the bowl in the microwave and cook on 'High' for two minutes. Check if the top of the mixture is firm. If it is not, cook for a few more seconds.

Step 5: Remove the container from the microwave and cut into sticks. Cut it while it is hot.

To make pumpkin porridge sticks:

Step 1: Combine oats, pumpkin puree, apple, pumpkin pie spice, and milk in a bowl. Allow them to soak for a few minutes, until very soft.

Step 2: Take a small, flat, microwave-safe container and spoon the oat mixture into it. Press the mixture onto the bottom of the container with the back of the spoon.

Step 3: Place the bowl in the microwave and cook on 'High' for two minutes. Check if the top of the mixture is firm. If it is not, cook for a few more seconds.

Step 4: Remove the container from the microwave and cut into sticks. Cut it while it is hot.

To make carrot porridge sticks:

Step 1: Combine oats, carrot, applesauce, ginger, cinnamon, nutmeg, and milk in a bowl. Allow them to soak for a few minutes, until very soft.

Step 2: Take a small, flat, microwave-safe container and spoon the oat mixture into it. Press the mixture onto the bottom of the container with the back of the spoon.

Step 3: Place the bowl in the microwave and cook on 'High' for two minutes. Check if the top of the mixture is firm. If it is not, cook for a few more seconds.

Step 4: Remove the container from the microwave and cut into sticks. Cut it while it is hot.

To make berry porridge sticks:

Step 1: Combine oats, vanilla, berries, and milk in a bowl. Allow them to soak for a few minutes,. until very soft.

Step 2: Take a small, flat, microwave-safe container and spoon the oat mixture into it. Press the mixture onto the bottom of the container with the back of the spoon.

Step 3: Place the bowl in the microwave and cook on 'High' for two minutes. Check if the top of the mixture is firm. If it is not, cook for a few more seconds.

Step 4: Remove the container from the microwave and cut into sticks. Cut it while it is hot.

Step 5: Serve warm. Put a porridge stick in your baby's hand and let them try to eat it themselves. If they are not able to, you go ahead and feed them.

Notes:

• Store leftover porridge sticks in an airtight container in the refrigerator.
• Make sure to use it within three days.
• Warm before serving.

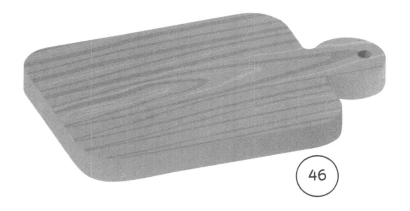

Makes: 2 baby servings
Age: 6 months +

Strawberry Quinoa Cereal

Ingredients:

¼ cup quinoa

¼ cup strawberries, hulled

A drop or two of vanilla extract

½ cup water or milk (you can use any milk of your choice like formula milk, breast milk, almond milk etc.)

⅛ teaspoon ground cinnamon

Directions:

Step 1: Combine quinoa and milk or water in a saucepan.

Step 2: Place the saucepan over medium heat. When the mixture starts boiling, lower the heat and cover the saucepan. Cook for about 8-9 minutes.

Step 3: Meanwhile, chop the strawberries into smaller pieces.

Step 4: Stir the strawberries into the quinoa.

Step 5: Add cinnamon and vanilla extract and mix well.

Step 6: Cook until the quinoa is cooked. Turn off the heat.

Step 7: You can serve this to your baby now if you like to serve it chunky but make sure to cool it before serving. If you want to serve it pureed, blend the mixture with an immersion blender until the texture you desire is achieved. You can add some more milk or water while blending.

Notes:

• You can replace strawberries with any other berries or fruit of your choice, like apples or pears etc.

• If you are ok with adding maple syrup, you can add a few drops.

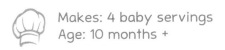

Brown Rice
Breakfast Pudding

Ingredients:

1 ½ cups cooked brown rice

1 inch stick cinnamon (You can use ground cinnamon instead of cinnamon stick if desired. You can add about 1/8 teaspoon of ground cinnamon or a bit more.)

½ cup pitted, finely chopped dates

⅛ cup raisins

cup unsweetened almond milk

A pinch ground cloves

½ Granny Smith apple, peeled and cored

Directions:

Step 1: Place rice, cinnamon, dates, and cloves in a saucepan.

Step 2: Pour milk into the saucepan and stir.

Step 3: Place the saucepan over medium-low heat and cook until the pudding is thick, making sure to stir frequently.

Step 4: Meanwhile, chop the apple into very small pieces. You can grate the apple as well.

Step 5: Finely chop the raisins.

Step 6: Turn off the heat.

Step 7: Discard the cinnamon stick (if using).

Step 8: Stir in apples and raisins and allow the mixture to cool until warm.

Step 9: Serve the required quantity and store the remaining in an airtight container in the refrigerator. It can store for up to three days.

Notes:

• To serve the stored pudding: Pour a little almond milk into a saucepan and the required quantity of the pudding. Heat the mixture over medium-low heat until warm.

Makes: 20 small pancakes or 10 regular-size pancakes
Age: 10 months +

Spinach Pancakes

Ingredients:

2 cups old fashioned oats
2 ripe bananas, sliced
1 cup milk of your choice
2 teaspoons ground cinnamon
2 teaspoons baking powder
2 cups packed spinach
2 eggs (or flax eggs)
2 tablespoons coconut oil, butter, or ghee
2 teaspoons vanilla extract
A pinch of salt (optional)

Directions:

Step 1: Add oats into a blender and grind until you get slightly smooth powder.

Step 2: Next add the bananas, spinach, oil, eggs, vanilla, cinnamon, and milk into the blender, and blend until the mixture is very smooth. Scrape the inner sides of the blender whenever required.

Step 3: Now add baking powder and salt, if using salt.

Step 4: Once you add the baking powder, mix on low speed for about 20 seconds.

Step 5: Pour the batter into a bowl.

Step 6: Place a non-stick pan over medium heat. When the pan is hot, pour about 2 to 3 tablespoons of the batter into the pan.

Step 7: Soon bubbles will be visible on the pancake. Cook until the underside is golden brown. Turn the pancake over and cook the other side evenly. Take out the pancake from the pan and keep warm.

Step 8: Repeat until the batter is done.

Step 9: You can cut a pancake into strips and serve it to your baby. Your baby would love to pick it up and eat. This is a great way to introduce greens to your baby.

50

Notes:

• If you want to use flax eggs, you need to make the flax eggs.

       • To make flax eggs: Take 2 tablespoons of flaxseed meal and combine it with 6 tablespoons of water.

• Keep it aside for 15 minutes. The mixture will become gel-like.

• You can add salt if you have no issues with giving salt to your baby.

       • You can also make a couple of pancakes for your baby and add salt to the remaining batter and make pancakes for your entire family.

• You can store leftover pancakes in an airtight container in the refrigerator. Make sure to use it within three to four days. Don't forget to heat the pancakes before serving.

Makes: 12 muffins
Age: 10 months +

Egg and Cheese Muffins

Ingredients:
⅛ cup grated onion or ½ teaspoon onion powder
4 eggs
½ cup shredded cheddar cheese
1 cup grated butternut squash, or carrot, or minced broccoli, or spinach
1 cup drained cottage cheese
¼ cup grated parmesan cheese

Directions:
Step 1: Preheat your oven to 350°F.
Step 2: Prepare two muffin pans of 12 counts each by greasing them with cooking spray. Place disposable liners if desired.
Step 3: rack the eggs into a bowl. Beat the eggs lightly.
Step 4: Add onion, cheese, the chosen vegetable, cottage cheese, and parmesan cheese to the eggs and stir until well combined.
Step 5: Divide the batter into the muffin cups. You can fill the batter right up to the top of the muffin cups.
Step 6: Place the muffin pans in the oven and bake for 15 to 25 minutes (depending on if you are using a mini-muffin pan or regular muffin pan) or until light golden brown on top and slightly hard on top. Bake them in batches if required.
Step 7: Take out the muffin pan from the oven and let them cool for a few minutes. Run a knife around the edges of the muffins to loosen them.
Step 8: Invert onto a plate. Serve warm.

Notes:
• You can also make mini-muffins using mini-muffin pans.
• These muffins are enjoyed by adults and babies alike.
• Store remaining muffins in an airtight container in the refrigerator. Use them within four to five days.

Makes: 1 baby serving
Age: 10 months +

Vegetable Smoothie

Ingredients:
½ cup milk of your choice
¼ cup fresh or frozen fruit of your choice
½ small banana, fresh or frozen

Choose any one vegetable:
¼ cup chopped kale
¼ cup chopped spinach
¼ cup chopped cauliflower
¼ cup sliced zucchini (fresh or frozen)
¼ cup sliced summer squash (fresh or frozen)
¼ cup roasted sweet potato
¼ cup roasted butternut squash
¼ cup steamed, diced beets

Optional ingredients (use any one):
½ teaspoon hemp seeds
½ teaspoon chia seeds
½ teaspoon ground flaxseeds
1 tablespoon chopped avocado
½-1 teaspoon cocoa powder
1 teaspoon maple syrup
½ tablespoon rolled oats
½ tablespoon nut butter (if you are willing to introduce nut butter)

Directions:
Step 1: Place banana and fruit in a blender.
Step 2: Add the chosen vegetable and optional ingredient if using.
Step 3: Pour milk into the blender.
Step 4: Blend the mixture until smooth. Scrape the inner sides of the blender if required.
Step 5: Add more milk if the smoothie is very thick.
Step 6: Serve right away.

Makes: 1 baby serving
Age: 10 months +

Scrambled Egg

Ingredients:
1 large egg
1 teaspoon butter
1 teaspoon plain Greek-style yogurt

Directions:
Step 1: Crack egg into a bowl.

Step 2: Add yogurt and whisk well in one direction with a fork.

Step 3: Melt butter in a medium skillet over medium-low heat.

Step 4: Add egg mixture and do not stir for about 10 seconds.

Step 5: Now lift the egg by moving a rubber spatula from underneath the outer edge of the egg and fold it over itself.

Step 6: Repeat this process from all over the remaining edges, each time folding over itself, towards the center.

Step 7: Transfer the scrambled egg onto a plate and serve immediately

Notes:
• The egg should be soft cooked yet set; your baby should be able to pick up the pile of egg chunks by himself/herself.

• You can add salt and pepper if you are serving toddlers.

LUNCH
RECIPES

Avocado Toast Plate

Ingredients:

1 slice whole grain toast

2 tablespoons mashed avocado

½ teaspoon hemp seeds

2-3 melon slices

¼ cup plain Greek-style yogurt or cottage cheese

Directions:

Step 1: Toast the bread slice in a toaster.

Step 2: Smear the avocado over the toasted bread slice.

Step 3: Cut into sticks.

Step 4: Scatter hemp seeds on top.

Step 5: Place the toast sticks on a plate. Place melon slices and yogurt alongside and serve.

Makes: 5-6 baby servings
Age: 6 months +

Roasted Sweet Potatoes

Ingredients:
½ tablespoon olive oil
2 large orange sweet potatoes or garnet yam
¼ teaspoon dried oregano (optional)
¼ teaspoon garlic powder (optional)

Directions:
Step 1: Prepare a baking sheet by lining it with parchment paper.
Step 2: Preheat the oven to 400°F.
Step 3: Peel the sweet potatoes and rinse well. Cut them into fries.
Step 4: Place sweet potato fries in a bowl.
Step 5: Drizzle oil over the sweet potatoes and toss well.
Step 6: Sprinkle garlic powder and oregano if using.
Step 7: Toss well.
Step 8: Transfer the seasoned fries to the baking sheet and spread in a single layer, without overlapping.
Step 9: Place the baking sheet in the oven and roast for about 20-25 minutes, or until fork tender.
You can give it to your baby in his/her hand as finger food and let them enjoy it by themselves.

Notes:
• You can start off initially without adding the spices when you start weaning. Once your • baby is familiar with sweet potatoes, you can add spices.
• For babies over a year old, you can sprinkle a bit of salt if desired.
• You can also puree this recipe with a little warm water if your baby is not happy with finger foods.
• Add a tablespoon of water initially and blend.
• Add more water according to the preferred consistency.
• Place leftover fries in an airtight container in the refrigerator.
• Make sure to consume within three to four days.

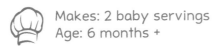

Blueberry Avocado
Smoothie Bowl

Ingredients:
½ cup fresh or frozen blueberries
½ cup full-fat yogurt
⅓ cup mashed avocado
1 banana, sliced
2 teaspoons flaxseed meal
½ cup baby oatmeal or rolled oats
½ cup water

Directions:
Step 1: Place blueberries, oats, banana, flaxseed meal, water, yogurt, and avocado in a blender.
Step 2: Blend until smooth.
Step 3: Pour into two bowls and serve. (You can serve one bowl to your baby and enjoy the other bowl yourself.)

Serves: 2 baby servings
Age: 6 months +

Vegetable Khichdi
(Rice with Lentils and Vegetables)

Ingredients:
¼ cup split yellow mung beans or red lentils
½ cup finely chopped vegetables like zucchini, carrot, potato, or green beans
¼ cup rice (preferably short grain white rice)
½ teaspoon ghee
¼ teaspoon cumin seeds
A pinch of turmeric powder
A tiny pinch of asafetida (optional but recommended)
2 cups water (plus extra to soak)

Directions:
Step 1: Combine lentils and rice in a bowl and rinse well.
Step 2: Pour enough water to cover the lentils and rice mixture. Let it soak for about an hour. Drain off the water.
Step 3: Preheat your saucepan, instant pot, pressure cooker, or rice cooker.
Step 4: Add ghee.
Step 5: When ghee melts and is slightly smoking, add cumin seeds.
Step 6: You will hear the cumin crackle when it's ready. Once it crackles, add turmeric and asafetida and stir for a few seconds.
Step 7: Add rice and lentil mixture along with two cups of water and the vegetables and stir. You can add more water if you want it watery.
Step 8: Mix well and cook the mixture until very soft.
Step 9: Cool for a few minutes and serve with plain yogurt.

Notes:
• If you have a pressure cooker, a rice cooker, or an instant pot, use it to make this recipe. You can also cook it in a saucepan, but it will take long to cook.
• When you are introducing this recipe to your baby, mash up the ingredients with a potato masher. After a week or so you can serve it the way it is cooked.
• Add salt for babies over a year old.
• This is a one pot dish for adults as well, just make sure to add salt for the adults.

Makes: 1 baby serving
Age: 6 months +

Apple and Ricotta
Plate

Ingredients:
¼ cup full-fat ricotta cheese
A pinch ground cinnamon
½ apple, peeled, cored and grated or sliced

Directions:
Step 1: Grate the apple.
Step 2: Combine ricotta, cinnamon, and grated apple in a bowl and serve.

Notes:
• You can steam the apples if desired.
• For babies over 8 months old, you can cut the apple into thin slices so that the baby holds the apple slices by hand.
• If your baby is over 8 months old, combine cinnamon and ricotta in a bowl. Give them apple slices to dip in the ricotta and enjoy.

Beef Stew

Ingredients:

4 ounces boneless beef chuck roast, cut into ½ inch cubes
⅛ small onion, chopped
½ medium Yukon gold potato, peeled, cut into 1 inch cubes
1 teaspoon olive oil
5 baby carrots, peeled and cut into 2-inch pieces
½ cup water (or more if required)

Directions:

Step 1: Pour oil into a heavy bottomed pan.
Step 2: Place the pan over medium-high heat.
Step 3: When the oil is hot, add beef and cook until the beef is brown all over.
Step 4: Add the vegetables and water to the pan.
Step 5: When the mixture begins to boil, lower the heat and cook covered until the meat and vegetables are soft. (It can take a long time to cook, about an hour or so.)
Step 6: Turn off the heat and blend with an immersion blender until the texture you desire is achieved. This blending is for the 6 month olds, only when you start off with weaning. Step 7: As your baby grows and your baby is able to eat chopped meat and vegetables you need not blend. You can cut the meat and vegetables into smaller pieces before cooking.
Step 8: Serve warm.

Notes:

• Store leftover stew in an airtight container in the refrigerator.
• Serve within three to four days.

Tuna Sandwich

Ingredients:

1-2 tablespoons mayonnaise
1 slice fresh bread
⅛ cup canned tuna in spring water

Directions:

Step 1: Remove the crust of the bread if desired and cut into two halves or triangles.

Step 2: Spread mayonnaise on one side of each half.

Step 3: Spread tuna on the other side of the bread halves.

Step 4: Combine the bread halves together so that the mayonnaise and tuna are touching..

Step 5: Serve.

Notes:

• You can also use frozen baby prawns instead of tuna. All you need to do is put the frozen prawns in a bowl of water for a few minutes to thaw. Once thawed, remove the prawns and mix them up with mayonnaise to use as a filling for the sandwich.

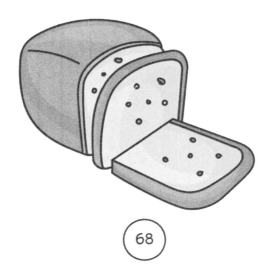

Makes: 1 baby serving
Age: 6 months +

Chicken Caesar Sandwich

Ingredients:
⅛ cup cooked, chopped chicken
2-3 tablespoons crème fraîche
⅛ teaspoon fresh lemon juice (or to taste)
½ clove garlic, peeled
1 teaspoon grated parmesan cheese
2-3 capers (optional)
1 slice bread

Directions:
Step 1: Remove the crust of the bread if desired and cut into two halves or triangles.
Step 2: Place chicken, crème fraiche, lemon juice, garlic, cheese, and capers (if using) in a blender and blend until the consistency you desire is achieved.
Step 3: Spread the mixture on one piece of bread. Cover with the other piece of bread and serve.

Chicken Clear Soup

Ingredients:
1 chicken thigh
¼ teaspoon coriander seeds
¼ teaspoon cumin seeds
¼ teaspoon grated ginger
½ onion, chopped
1 clove garlic, peeled and sliced
½ teaspoon unsalted butter
½ tomato, chopped
1 cup water

Directions:
Step 1: Add butter into a saucepan and place the saucepan over medium heat.
Step 2: Once butter melts, add cumin and coriander seeds.
Step 3: Once the cumin crackles, add in the garlic, ginger, and onion.
Step 4: Cook for a couple of minutes until the onion turns pink.
Step 5: Add tomato and mix well.
Step 6: Cook until soft.
Step 7: Stir in the chicken and cook for about four minutes.
Step 8: Pour water into the pot and stir.
Step 9: When the soup starts boiling, lower the heat and cook until the chicken is tender.
Step 10: Strain the soup and serve.

Notes:
• Discard the solids.
• As your baby grows older, you can blend the soup without straining, until chunky.

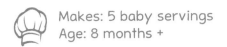
Healthy Mac N' Cheese

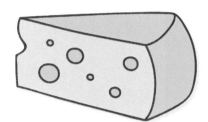

Ingredients:
½ medium butternut squash, deseeded
½ tablespoon olive oil
1 clove garlic, peeled and minced
¼ teaspoon mild curry powder
¼ cup grated parmesan cheese (optional)
6 ounces small sized pasta
¼ yellow onion, diced
½ cup chicken or vegetable broth
½ teaspoon chopped fresh thyme, sage, or rosemary (optional)

Directions:
Step 1: Prepare a baking sheet by lining it with parchment paper.
Step 2: Preheat your oven to 400°F.
Step 3: Place butternut squash on the prepared baking sheet with the skin side down.
Step 4: Place the baking sheet in the oven and roast for 40 minutes, or until fork tender.
Step 5: Take out the baking sheet from the oven and let it completely cool.
Step 6: While the squash is cooking, cook the pasta following the instructions given on the package.
Step 7: Pour oil into a skillet and let it heat over medium heat. Add onion and cook until translucent.
Step 8: Stir in garlic and cook for about a minute or until you get a nice fragrance in the air.
Step 9: Using a spoon, scoop out the butternut squash pulp and add into a blender.
Step 10: Add the cooked garlic and onion, curry powder, thyme, and broth into the blender and blend until very smooth.
Step 11: Pour the blended mixture into the skillet.
Step 12: Stir in pasta.
Step 13: Add cheese and stir. Turn off the heat.
Step 14: Take out as much as required for your baby. Add salt and pepper to taste to the remaining pasta and enjoy it with your family.

Notes:
• Store the remaining portion in an airtight container in the refrigerator. Use it within four days.

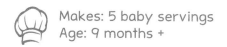

Rice Soup with Veggies

Ingredients:

4 cups chicken broth, unsalted
1 small green onion or leek, thinly sliced
1 carrot, peeled and grated
8 ounces mixed greens of your choice like: spinach, green or red cabbage, kale, broccoli, Brussels sprouts etc. finely chopped
½ cup rice, rinsed well
½ tablespoon extra-virgin olive oil to serve, for each serving (optional)
½ tablespoon grated parmesan cheese to serve, for each serving (optional)
½ tablespoon minced parsley

Directions:

Step 1: If you have time, soak the rice in water for about an hour.
Step 2: Place a saucepan over medium heat.
Step 3: Add a tablespoon of broth.
Step 4: Add carrot and leek and sauté for a couple of minutes.
Step 5: Add remaining broth and mixed green vegetables.
Step 6: When the mixture begins to boil, add rice and stir.
Step 7: Lower the heat and cook until the rice is soft.
Step 8: Turn off the heat.

Step 9: Add parsley and stir. When you introduce this to your baby for the first time, it is better to blend the soup slightly. So take out as much as required and blend the soup.
Step 10: Serve each serving with a little parmesan cheese and olive oil if desired.

Notes:

• The remaining soup can be enjoyed by you and your family. Make sure to add salt and pepper for you and your family.
• Store leftover soup in an airtight container in the refrigerator. It can last for about three days.

Pumpkin Risotto

Makes: five baby servings
Age: 9 months +

Ingredients:
2 cups chicken or vegetable broth
1 tablespoon unsalted butter or olive oil
1 clove garlic, peeled and minced
¾ cup Arboro rice, rinsed
⅛ teaspoon ground nutmeg
½ cup canned or cooked pumpkin puree
¼ white onion, minced
½ teaspoon dried thyme
¼ cup grated parmesan cheese
Black pepper to taste (optional)

Directions:
Step 1: Combine broth and pumpkin puree in a saucepan.
Step 2: Place the saucepan over high heat.
Step 3: Keep stirring until the stock is well combined with the puree.
Step 4: When the mixture begins to boil, lower the heat and let it simmer.
Step 5: Meanwhile, add butter into another saucepan and place the saucepan over medium heat.
Step 6: Once the butter melts, add in the garlic and onion, and cook until the onion turns translucent.
Step 7: Mix in the rice and thyme. Stir for a couple of minutes until the rice turns opaque.
Step 8: Pour about ½ cup of the simmering stock into the saucepan and stir. Cook until the broth is absorbed.
Step 9: Repeat the previous step of adding broth, half cup at a time, and cook until all of the broth is absorbed.
Step 10: After adding all of the broth, if the rice is still not cooked, add some more broth. Step 11: Make sure to heat the stock before adding. Cook until rice is creamy.
Step 12: Stir in parmesan cheese and nutmeg. Add pepper to taste. Turn off the heat.
Step 13: You can serve it with some toppings of your baby's choice.

Notes:
• You can serve this dish to your baby if they are able to eat it this way; otherwise, blend the risotto to the desired texture and feed your baby.
• Once you feed your baby, you can add salt and pepper to taste and feed the rest of your family.
• If you have any leftovers, place them in an airtight container after they have cooled completely. Keep it refrigerated and consume within five days.
• Reheat before serving.

Summer Pesto Finger Salad

Ingredients:
¼ cup dry orzo pasta
⅛ cup frozen corn, thawed
1 tablespoon pesto
⅛ cup finely chopped zucchini
⅛ cup deseeded, finely chopped tomatoes

Directions:
Step 1: Pour water into a small saucepan, filling it up to ¾ with water, and place the saucepan over high heat.
Step 2: When water starts boiling, add the orzo.
Step 3: After six minutes, drop the zucchini and corn into the saucepan with the orzo and cook for a minute or two.
Step 4: Drain well in a colander and rinse under cold running water.
Step 5: Add the orzo with vegetables into a bowl.
Step 6: Add tomatoes to the same bowl and toss well.
Step 7: Drizzle pesto and toss well.
Step 8: You can serve as it is or heat it up slightly and serve.

Notes:
• You can use homemade pesto or store-bought pesto.

Curry Pasta Salad

Ingredients:
½ cup small size dry pasta
2 small broccoli florets, finely chopped
1 baby carrot, finely chopped
A small handful chickpeas (canned or cooked)

For dressing:
⅛ cup plain yogurt
¾ teaspoon olive oil
¼ teaspoon mild curry powder
⅛ teaspoon ground ginger
⅛ teaspoon garlic powder
¾ teaspoon apple cider vinegar
¼ teaspoon agave nectar (optional)
1/8 teaspoon turmeric powder

Optional ingredients:
½ cup chopped or shredded, cooked chicken
½ cup finely chopped golden raisins
1 tablespoon minced fresh parsley
⅛ cup finely chopped zucchini

Directions:
Step 1: Peel the skin off the chickpeas and chop them into smaller pieces.
Step 2: Cook pasta following the instructions given on the package, but add carrot, chickpeas, and broccoli while cooking the pasta. (Also add zucchini if using.)
Step 3: Drain and set aside to cool in a bowl.
Step 4: To make dressing: Whisk together yogurt, oil, apple cider vinegar, spices and agave nectar in a bowl.
Step 5: Add a little of the dressing into the bowl of pasta.
Step 6: Toss well.
Step 7: Check if your baby will be able to handle the taste. Add more dressing if desired.
Step 8: Take out as much as required for your baby and serve.
Step 9: To the remaining salad, add the rest of the dressing and some salt and pepper to taste. You can add more curry powder if desired.
Step 10: Toss well and serve the rest to your family.

Makes: 6-8 adult servings or 12-16 baby servings
Age: 10 months +

Chicken Pasta Soup

Ingredients:
½ tablespoon olive oil
3 medium carrots, finely chopped
3 cloves garlic, minced
2 ribs celery, very thinly sliced
½ teaspoon fresh minced thyme or ¼ teaspoon dry thyme
1 bay leaf
1 cup small size pasta, preferably whole wheat
½ small onion, chopped
6 cups unsalted or low sodium chicken broth
¾ pound boneless, skinless chicken breast
Minced parsley to garnish

Directions:
Step 1: Pour oil into a soup pot and place the soup pot over medium heat.
Step 2: Once the oil is hot, add onion, garlic, carrots, and celery and stir. Cook until the onion turns translucent.
Step 3: Stir in the thyme and cook for a few seconds, or until you get a nice aroma.
Step 4: Pour broth into the mixture and stir. (Scrape the bottom of the pot to remove any browned bits that may be stuck.)
Step 5: Add the bay leaf and raise the heat to high heat.
Step 6: When the mixture starts boiling, add the chicken.
Step 7: Lower the heat and cook for about 15 minutes.
Step 8: Drop the pasta into the pot and cook until the pasta and chicken are both fully cooked.
Step 9: Turn off the heat.
Step 10: Take the chicken out of the pot and shred it with a pair of forks. (You can also chop into small pieces.)
Step 11: Add the shredded/cut chicken back into the pot.
Step 12: Take out as much as soup required for your baby and add salt and pepper to the rest of the soup for you and your family to enjoy.
Step 13: You can garnish with parsley when you serve.

VEGETARIAN DINNER RECIPES

Lentil and Pumpkin
Soup

Ingredients:
⅛ cup red lentils, rinsed well
½ cup cubed pumpkin
½ small onion, chopped
1 small carrot, peeled and cut into ¼ inch cubes
2 cloves garlic, minced
½ teaspoon ghee (or butter)
3 cups water
Pepper to taste (optional)

Directions:
Step 1: Add ghee (or butter) into a heavy pot and heat over medium heat.
Step 2: When ghee or butter melts, add onion and garlic and stir. Cook for a couple of minutes until the onion turns translucent.
Step 3: Add carrot, pumpkin, lentils, and water.
Step 4: When the mixture begins to boil, lower the heat and cook covered until the lentils are soft.
Step 5: Let it cool completely
Step 6: You can either blend the soup, mash it with a potato masher, or serve it as it is, depending on the age of your baby.

Notes:
• You can store the leftover soup in the refrigerator. Make sure to consume within four days.

Vegetable Soup

Ingredients:

1 small potato, peeled and cubed
4 green beans, thinly sliced
2 small carrots, peeled and sliced
6 broccoli florets, finely chopped
½ inch piece ginger, peeled and grated
7-8 button mushrooms, finely chopped
½ onion, finely chopped
2 teaspoons butter (or ghee)
2-3 cups water
Pepper to taste
¼ teaspoon ground cumin
¼ cup milk of your choice

Directions:

Step 1: Melt butter in a soup pot over medium heat.
Step 2: When butter melts, add onion and cook until soft.
Step 3: Stir in ginger and cook for a couple of minutes.
Step 4: Add all of the vegetables and stir for three minutes.
Step 5: Add water and let it come to a boil.
Step 6: Lower the heat and cook until the vegetables are soft.
Step 7: Add milk and pepper and stir.
Step 8: Serve.

Notes:

• For a start, you can puree the vegetables and serve. As your baby grows, stop pureeing the vegetables.
• You can serve the remaining soup to your family adding some more pepper and some salt.

Makes: 1 baby serving
Age: 6 months +

Cheese
and Vegetable Supper

Ingredients:

1 tablespoon hot milk
⅛ cup cooked green peas
⅛ cup finely grated mild cheddar cheese
¼ cup cottage cheese
3 tablespoons cream cheese
½ tablespoon chopped carrot, cooked, hot
A large pinch parmesan cheese

Directions:

Step 1: Add cream cheese, cottage cheese, cheddar cheese, and milk into a bowl and whisk until smooth.
Step 2: Add carrots and stir.
Step 3: Garnish with parmesan cheese and serve.

Makes: 5 baby servings
Age: 6 months +

Sweet Corn and Sweet Potato
Pasta

Ingredients:

1 pound sweet potatoes, peeled and chopped
½ pound cauliflower, cut into small florets
2.5-3 ounces grated cheese
1 ¼ cups whole milk
2.8 frozen sweet corn
¼ cup cooked pasta to serve

Directions:

Step 1: Combine milk and sweet potatoes in a saucepan.
Step 2: Place the saucepan over medium heat and let the mixture come to a boil.
Step 3: Lower the heat and cook for about eight minutes.
Step 4: Add cauliflower and let it cook for an additional 10 minutes.
Step 5: Mix corn into the saucepan and let it cook for about five minutes.
Step 6: Turn off the heat.
Step 7: Add cheese and blend the mixture with an immersion blender until the texture you desire is achieved.
Step 8: Pour into an airtight container. Refrigerate until use. Make sure to use it within five days.

Notes:

• For a 6 month old baby, add pasta into the blender. Add some of the sauce and blend to the desired consistency.
• For older babies, mix the sauce with cooked pasta and serve.

Makes: 6 baby servings
Age: 6 months +

Butternut Squash Creamy Pasta

Ingredients:
½ small butternut squash, peeled, deseeded, and chopped into chunks
½ medium onion, finely chopped
A pinch black pepper
½ tablespoon plain yogurt
1 tablespoon olive oil
1 clove garlic, peeled and minced
¼ cup vegetable stock or water
1 teaspoon butter

Directions:
Step 1: Preheat the oven to 350°F.
Step 2: Place butternut squash on a baking sheet.
Step 3: Drizzle oil over the squash.
Step 4: Place the baking sheet in the oven and roast until soft. It should take around 30 to 40 minutes. Set aside.
Step 5: Place a pan over medium heat.
Step 6: Add butter.
Step 7: When butter melts, add onion and cook until light brown.
Step 8: Stir in garlic and cook for a couple of minutes. Stir often.
Step 9: Stir in the roasted butternut squash, pepper, and yogurt, and lower the heat.
Step 10: Cook for eight minutes.
Step 11: Turn off the heat and let it cool for a few minutes.
Step 12: Transfer the mixture into a blender and blend until smooth.
Step 13: Meanwhile, follow the instructions given on the package of pasta and cook the pasta.
Step 14: Transfer the pasta into a bowl.
Step 15: Add the blended sauce and toss well.
Step 16: Serve your baby.

Notes:
• You can serve the remaining portion to your family by adding some salt and pepper.
• You can also store the sauce and pasta in separate airtight containers in the refrigerator. • Make sure to use it within four days.
• Combine the pasta and sauce in a pan and heat it up before serving.

Potato, Carrot, and Sweet Corn
Balls

Ingredients:
½ medium potato, peeled and cubed
½ medium carrot, peeled and cubed
1 small onion, finely chopped
2 tablespoons fresh breadcrumbs
½ teaspoon minced fresh thyme
1 tablespoon grated cheddar cheese
¼ teaspoon sweet chili sauce (optional)
Flour to dredge
Cooking oil spray

Directions:
Step 1: Steam the carrot and potatoes until soft.
Step 2: Let them cool completely.
Step 3: Place the carrots and potatoes in a bowl and mash well.
Step 4: Add onion, breadcrumbs, thyme, cheddar cheese, and chili sauce if using. Mix well.
Step 5: Make 8-9 balls of the mixture. Place some flour on a plate. Dredge the balls in flour.
Step 6: Place a non-stick pan over medium heat. Spray the pan with cooking spray.
Step 7: Place the balls in the pan and cook until golden brown all over. Spray some oil over the balls if required.
Step 8: Serve.

Notes:
• You can make the balls and store them in freezer-safe bags in the freezer.
• Thaw the balls and heat in an oven or pan before serving.

Makes: 1 baby serving
Age: 6 months +

Banana Sandwich

Ingredients:
1 slice fresh bread
½ ripe banana

Directions:
Step 1: Remove the crust from the bread slice and cut it into two halves or triangles.
Step 2: Mash the banana well using a fork and spread it on one half of the bread slice.
Step 3: Cover with the other half of the bread slice and serve.

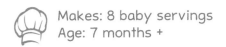
Vegetable Risotto

Ingredients:
3 cups vegetable broth or stock
2 teaspoons unsalted butter
1 cup Arborio rice, rinsed
½ onion, minced
2 cups grated, mixed vegetables like zucchini, carrot, broccoli etc.
¼ cup grated parmesan cheese

Directions:
Step 1: Pour broth/stock into a saucepan.
Step 2: Place the saucepan over high heat.
Step 3: When the stock begins to boil, lower the heat and let it simmer.
Step 4: Meanwhile, add the butter into another saucepan and place the saucepan over medium heat.
Step 5: Once the butter melts, add onion and cook until onion turns clear.
Step 6: Mix in the rice. Stir for a couple of minutes until the rice turns opaque.
Step 7: Add vegetables and stir.
Step 8: Pour about ½ cup of the simmering broth/stock into the saucepan and stir.
Step 9: Cook until the stock is absorbed.
Step 10: Repeat the previous step of adding broth/stock, half cup at a time, and cook until stock is absorbed, until all the broth/stock is added. Stir often.
Step 11: After adding all of the broth/stock, if the rice is still not cooked, add some more broth/stock. Make sure to heat the broth/stock before adding. Cook until the rice is creamy.
Step 12: Stir in the parmesan cheese and nutmeg.
Step 13: Turn off the heat.
Step 14: You can serve it to your baby if he/she is able to eat it this way. Otherwise, blend the risotto to the desired texture and feed your baby.
Step 15: Once you feed your baby, you can add salt and pepper to taste and feed the rest of your family.
Step 16: If you have any leftovers, place them in an airtight container, after cooling completely. Keep them refrigerated and consume within five days. Reheat before serving.

Avocado Soup

Ingredients:

3 ounces homemade, unsalted vegetable stock (warmed)
1 ounce milk of your choice
½ ripe avocado, peeled, pitted, and mashed
½ teaspoon minced fresh cilantro

Directions:

Step 1: Combine vegetable stock and avocado in a bowl.
Step 2: Stir in milk.
Step 3: Garnish with cilantro and serve.

Notes:

• You can use any milk, including formula or breast milk.

Makes: 1-2 baby servings
Age: 8 months +

Chickpea and Red Pepper
Couscous

Ingredients:
5 ounces very low-sodium vegetable stock
1.8 ounces couscous
¼ red bell pepper, chopped
¼ small onion, chopped
1 tablespoon unsalted butter
½ tablespoon olive oil
1.8 ounces cooked or canned chickpeas

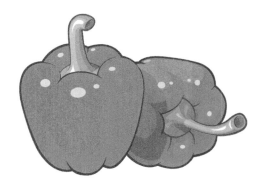

Directions:
Step 1: Pour stock into a pan.
Step 2: Place the pan over medium heat.
Step 3: When stock begins to boil, stir in the butter.
Step 4: When the butter melts, add couscous, and stir.
Step 5: Turn off the heat and keep it aside for six minutes.
Step 6: Take a fork and fluff the couscous.
Step 7: Add chickpeas to a microwave-safe bowl.
Step 8: Pour enough water into the bowl to cover the chickpeas.
Step 9: Cook on 'High' for about two minutes.
Step 10: Drain off the water from the chickpeas.
Step 11: Place another pan over medium heat. Add oil. When oil is hot, add onion and cook until translucent.
Step 12: Stir in bell pepper and chickpeas and cook for a couple of minutes.
Step 13: Add couscous and mix well.
Step 14: Turn off the heat and serve to your baby.

Notes:
• Once you are done with serving your baby, add some lemon juice, salt, and pepper (to taste) and serve your family.

Spaghetti Bolognese

Ingredients:
½ tablespoon olive oil
1 small carrot, grated
5-6 mushrooms, finely chopped
4.4 ounces frozen soya mince
½ teaspoon dried mixed herbs, or ½ teaspoon minced fresh basil
2 tablespoons grated cheese
½ medium onion, finely chopped
½ orange bell pepper, deseeded and finely chopped
8.8 ounces tomato puree
½ cube very low salt vegetable stock cube, crumbled
4.4 ounces spaghetti

Directions:
Step 1: Pour oil into a pan.
Step 2: Place the pan over medium heat.
Step 3: Once oil is hot, add onion and cook for about a minute.
Step 4: Add carrot and bell pepper and mix well.
Step 5: Cook for about five minutes, or until slightly tender.
Step 6: Stir in mushrooms and cook for a couple of minutes.
Step 7: Mix in the soya mince, tomato puree, crumbled stock cube, and mixed herbs, and mix well. Cook until the sauce is thick.
Step 8: While the sauce is thickening, prepare the pasta. Follow the instructions given on the package of pasta.
Step 9: Once you drain the spaghetti, cut it into smaller pieces.
Step 10: Add some sauce and toss well.
Step 11: Garnish with cheese and serve.

Notes:
• The remaining sauce and spaghetti can be enjoyed by you and your family. Don't forget to add some salt.

Makes: 2-3 baby servings
Age: 9 months +

Sweet Corn Soup

Ingredients:
1 cup corn kernels
⅛ teaspoon turmeric powder
⅛ teaspoon grated ginger
⅛ teaspoon grated garlic
½ cup finely chopped mixed vegetables (carrot, peas, and green beans)
¼ teaspoon butter (or ghee)
A pinch pepper
2 cups water

Directions:
Step 1: Steam the corn kernels until soft.
Step 2: Once the kernels have cooled, transfer them into a blender. Add a little water and blend until smooth.
Step 3: Steam the mixed vegetables.
Step 4: Add ghee to a saucepan over medium heat.
Step 5: When ghee melts, add ginger, garlic, and turmeric, and cook for a few seconds.
Step 6: Add the blended corn and vegetables and the remaining water, and stir
Step 7: When the soup starts boiling, turn off the heat.
Step 8: Add pepper and stir.
Step 9: Serve. Once you serve your baby, you can add salt and pepper to taste and enjoy it with your family.

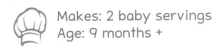

Makes: 2 baby servings
Age: 9 months +

Macaroni Cheese
with Broccoli and Cauliflower

Ingredients:
⅛ cup cauliflower florets
⅛ cup broccoli florets
1.8 ounces macaroni
1 tablespoon plain white flour
½ – ¾ cup skimmed milk
¼ teaspoon mustard powder
½ tablespoon butter
½ bay leaf
2 tablespoons grated cheddar cheese + extra to top

Directions:
Step 1: Steam the broccoli and cauliflower florets until tender.
Step 2: Once cooked, chop the broccoli and cauliflower into smaller pieces.
Step 3: Cook the macaroni following the instructions given on the package of the pasta.
Step 4: Meanwhile, place a saucepan over medium heat. Add butter. When butter melts, add flour and keep stirring until a roux is formed.
Step 5: Stir in the bay leaf to the roux.
Step 6: Stirring constantly, add ¼ of the milk.
Step 7: When the sauce becomes slightly thick, add another ¼ of the milk. (Make sure to stir all the while.)
Step 8: Repeat this process until the remaining milk is added.
Step 9: Add mustard powder and cheese, and stir. Turn off the heat.
Step 10: Add pasta, broccoli, and cauliflower, and mix well.
Step 11: Preheat the oven to 425°F.
Step 12: Spoon the pasta into a baking dish.
Step 13: Top with some cheddar cheese.
Step 14: Place the baking dish in the oven and bake until golden brown on top.
Step 15: You can cut the mac and cheese (just sufficient for your baby) into smaller pieces and serve.

Notes:
• Add some salt and pepper to the rest and enjoy it with your family.
• You can add any other vegetables of your choice instead of broccoli and cauliflower.

Pea Fritters

Ingredients:

1 ½ cups frozen peas
¾ cup self-raising or plain flour
3 tablespoons crumbled feta cheese
1 large egg
⅛ cup sliced green onion
1 tablespoon chopped parsley (or any other fresh
herbs of your choice)
Oil to fry as required

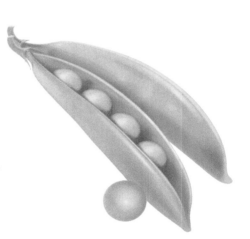

Directions:

Step 1: Cook peas in a pot of water for four minutes.

Step 2: Drain the peas and place in a food processor.

Step 3: Add flour, spring onion, and egg, and give short pulses until well incorporated.

Step 4: Add the blended mixture into a bowl.

Step 5: Add cheese and parsley and mix well.

Step 6: Place a non-stick pan over medium heat. Add a little oil or use some cooking spray.

Step 7: Drop a tablespoon of the mixture on the pan and flatten it slightly. Place as many fritters as required for your baby in the pan.

Step 8: Cook until the underside is golden brown. Turn the fritters over and cook the other side until golden brown.

Step 9: Serve.

Notes:

• To the remaining mixture add some salt and pepper to taste and cook the fritters. These are for you and your family to enjoy.

Makes: 6-8 baby servings
Age: 10 months +

Healthy Pizza

Ingredients:
2 sweet potatoes, rinsed
Low-sodium tomato sauce, as required
Grated mozzarella cheese, as required
Olive oil to brush

Directions:
Step 1: Prepare a baking sheet by lining it with parchment paper or aluminum foil.
Step 2: Preheat the oven to 425°F.
Step 3: Dry the sweet potatoes with paper towels.
Step 4: Brush olive oil all over the sweet potatoes and place them on the baking sheet.
Step 5: Place the baking sheet in the oven and bake for about 40 to 45 minutes, or until the sweet potatoes are fork tender.
Step 6: Take out the baking sheet and cool the sweet potatoes completely.
Step 7: Once you are able to handle the sweet potatoes, cut them into thick round slices. Step 8: Do not peel them.
Step 9: Place the slices on the baking sheet and spread some tomato sauce over them.
Step 10: Sprinkle mozzarella on top.
Step 11: Place the baking sheet in the oven and bake until the cheese melts and is bubbling.
Step 12: Take out the baking sheet from the oven. Peel off the skin from the sweet potato and serve.
Step 13: Once you have served your baby, you can serve the remaining to the rest of your family.

Notes:
• If you do not want to use low-sodium tomato sauce, you can use unsalted tomato sauce or blend some tomatoes and use it instead.
• Season with salt, pepper, oregano, and red chili flakes for you and your family.

Vegan Dinner
Recipes

Makes: 2-3 servings
Age: 7 months +

"Cheesy" Polenta

Ingredients:
¼ cup dried polenta
1 cup water
1-2 tablespoons nutritional yeast
1 teaspoon mild curry powder (or 1-2 teaspoons mixed spices and dried herbs of your choice)

Directions:
Step 1: Boil water in a heavy saucepan. Once water starts boiling, add polenta and stir.
Step 2: Lower the heat to medium-low and stir often until the polenta is cooked. If the mixture is very thick and not cooked, you can add some more water or non-dairy milk of your choice.
Step 3: Stir in the nutritional yeast and spice mix.
Step 4: Cook for three minutes before taking the saucepan off the heat.
Step 5: It is ready to serve to your baby if you want to serve it with a spoon. Take out as much as required for your baby and add into a bowl. Cool it slightly and serve.

Notes:
• If you want to serve it as finger food, spoon the polenta into a glass dish. Spread it evenly and smoothly. Let it cool completely.
• Store leftovers in an airtight container in the refrigerator. Make sure to use it within four days.
• In case you want to serve it to the rest of your family, add salt to the polenta after taking out a sufficient amount for your baby. Mix well and go to step 6.

Apple Carrot Soup

Ingredients:
½ cup peeled, cored, and cubed apple
½ cup peeled and cubed carrot
½ cup peeled and cubed potatoes
1 cup water
Large pinch ground cinnamon

Directions:
Step 1: Steam potato and carrot cubes for 10 minutes.
Step 2: Place the apple cubes along with the vegetables in the steaming basket.
Step 3: Continue steaming until the vegetables are tender.
Step 4: Let the mixture cool for a few minutes.
Step 5: Place apple, carrot, and potato cubes into a blender and blend the soup to the desired texture. (Add water according to the desired consistency.)
Step 6: Serve warm in bowls garnished with cinnamon.

Makes: 2-3 baby servings
Age: 6 months +

Green Puree

Ingredients:

3.5 ounces fresh or frozen peas

3.5 ounces fresh kale, torn (discard hard stem and ribs)

½ medium zucchini, chopped into pieces

Directions:

Step 1: Add peas, kale, and zucchini into a saucepan.

Step 2: Pour enough water into the saucepan to cover the vegetables.

Step 3: Place the saucepan over medium heat and cook until the vegetables are tender.

Step 4: Drain in a colander.

Step 5: Transfer the vegetables into a blender and blend until the texture you desire is achieved.

Notes:

• You can swap kale with any other greens of your choice.

• You can swap peas for broad beans or any other green vegetable of your choice.

• You can swap zucchini with broccoli or cauliflower.

Curried Butternut Squash Soup

Ingredients:
½ butternut squash, peeled, deseeded, and chopped into chunks
½ large white onion, chopped
1 inch ginger, peeled and thinly sliced
2 tablespoons canola oil
3 cloves garlic, crushed
1 teaspoon ground cumin
1 teaspoon ground coriander
½ teaspoon turmeric powder
½ tablespoons chopped tomatoes
4 ounces canned, chopped tomatoes
3 pods green cardamom
¾ cup coconut milk
⅓ cup milk
⅓ cup water
½ ripe mango, peeled and cut into small cubes
2 tablespoons tahini

Directions:
Step 1: Preheat the oven to 350°F.
Step 2: Place butternut squash on a baking sheet.
Step 3: Drizzle ½ tablespoon of oil over the squash.
Step 4: Place the baking sheet in the oven and roast until soft. It should take around 30 to 40 minutes.
Step 5: Place a pan over medium heat.
Step 6: Add remaining oil to the pan.
Step 7: When the oil is hot, add onion and cook until translucent.
Step 8: Stir in the ginger and garlic and cook for a couple of minutes, until you get a nice aroma.
Step 9: Stir in the cumin, coriander, cardamom, and turmeric powder. Cook for a few seconds.
Step 10: Add tomato puree, tomatoes, tahini, milk, water, and coconut milk, and mix well.
Step 11: When the mixture starts simmering, turn off the heat.
Step 12: By now the butternut squash would have cooked. Let the squash and tomato mixture cool for a few minutes.
Step 13: Now add mango, squash, and tomato mixture into a blender. Blend until the soup is smooth.
Step 14: Serve warm. Once you have taken out your baby's portion, you can serve the remaining to your family, adding some salt.

Broccoli Soup

Ingredients:
1 small onion, chopped
½ tablespoon olive oil
Water to cook, as required
½ cup chopped baby carrots (optional)
½ head broccoli, cut into florets
A large pinch of garlic powder

Directions:
Step 1: Place a saucepan over medium heat.
Step 2: Add oil and let it heat.
Step 3: Add onion and carrot and cook until slightly tender.
Step 4: Stir in the broccoli.
Step 5: Pour enough water to just cover the vegetables. (Do not submerge the vegetables in water fully; it should barely cover the vegetables, or else your soup will be very thin.)
Step 6: When the soup starts boiling, lower the heat and cook until the broccoli turns bright green in color.
Step 7: Turn off the heat.
Step 8: Stir in the garlic powder.
Step 9: Blend with an immersion blender until the texture you desire is achieved.
Step 10: Serve the required quantity to your baby and enjoy the rest yourself adding a little salt and pepper to taste.

Notes:
• In case you want to freeze the soup, pour into an ice cube tray and freeze until firm. Transfer the frozen cubes into freezer bags and freeze. Use within a month.
• To use frozen soup: Remove the required number of frozen cubes and place in a saucepan. • Let them thaw completely. Warm the soup and serve.

Quinoa and Peas

Ingredients:
1 ½ cups cooked quinoa
A handful frozen green peas, thawed
½ cup vegetable stock (or water)

Directions:
Step 1: Follow the instructions on the package of quinoa and cook the quinoa.

Step 2: Measure out 1 ½ cups of cooked quinoa and add into a saucepan.

Step 3: Also add peas and stock into the saucepan, and stir.

Step 4: Place the saucepan over medium heat and let the mixture cook for about eight minutes, stirring often.

Step 5: Turn off the heat and take out the required quantity for your baby; let it cool until warm, and serve.

Step 6: To the rest of the quinoa, add some seasonings to taste and enjoy it with your family dinner.

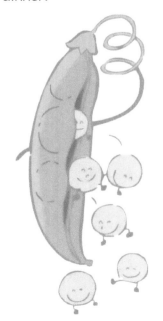

Pea and Mint Risotto

Makes: 3-4 baby servings
Age: 6 months +

Ingredients:
½ tablespoon olive oil
1 clove garlic, peeled and minced
¼ teaspoon dried oregano
2 cups unsalted vegetable stock (or water)
0.9-1 ounce grated vegan parmesan cheese (or nutritional yeast)
½ onion, minced
4.4 ounces Arborio rice, rinsed well
½ bay leaf
½ teaspoon minced fresh mint leaves
1 tablespoon dairy-free butter (optional)
Pepper to taste

Directions:
Step 1: Pour oil into a heavy saucepan and let it heat over medium heat.
Step 2: When oil is hot, add onion and cook until soft. Stir occasionally.
Step 3: Add garlic and mix well. Cook for about a minute or until you get a nice aroma.
Step 4: Meanwhile, heat the stock and let it simmer over low heat.
Step 5: To the saucepan with the onion and garlic, stir in the bay leaf, oregano, and rice. Cook, stirring frequently, for a couple of minutes, or until the rice turns opaque.
Step 6: Pour about ½ cup of the simmering stock into the saucepan and stir. Cook until the stock is absorbed.
Step 7: Repeat the previous step of adding stock, half cup at a time, and cook until stock is absorbed, until all the stock is added. Stir often.
Step 8: When you are adding stock for the last time, add peas, cheese, and mint.
Step 9: After adding all the stock, if the rice is still not cooked, add some more stock. Make sure to heat the stock before adding. Cook until rice is creamy.
Step 10: Turn off the heat. Discard the bay leaf.
Step 11: You can serve it to your baby if they are able to eat it this way; otherise, blend the risotto to the desired texture and feed it to your baby.
Step 12: Once you have fed your baby, you can add salt and pepper to taste and feed the rest of your family.

Notes:
• You can slightly mash the peas before adding to the risotto if you are serving to a 6 months old baby.
• If you have any leftovers, place them in an airtight container after cooling completely. Keep refrigerated and consume within five days. Reheat before serving.

Makes: 2-3 baby servings
Age: 7 months +

Tofu Nuggets

Ingredients:
½ block extra-firm tofu
½ tablespoon arrowroot powder
⅛ teaspoon mild chili powder
½ tablespoon extra-virgin olive oil
⅛ teaspoon garlic powder
⅛ teaspoon paprika (optional)

Directions:
Step 1: Preheat your oven to 400°F.
Step 2: Grease a baking sheet with cooking spray.
Step 3: Cut the tofu into the desired shape. (Cut it such that your baby can hold a piece of tofu.)
Step 4: Toss tofu with oil in a bowl.
Step 5: Dust oiled tofu with arrowroot powder, chili powder, garlic powder, and paprika (if using), and toss lightly until tofu is coated well.
Step 6: Spread the tofu evenly over the baking sheet.
Step 7: Place the baking sheet in the oven and bake for about 15 minutes. Turn the tofu slices over and bake for another 10-15 minutes.
Step 8: Cool slightly and serve to your baby.

Notes:
• If you want crispy nuggets, you need to remove extra moisture from the tofu.
• To remove extra moisture from the tofu, cut the tofu into 2-3 horizontal slices.
• Place a tofu slice over 1-2 layers of paper towels.
• Stack another tofu over the paper towels.
• Place some more layers of paper towels over the tofu.
• Repeat until all the tofu slices are placed on the stack.
• Cover with paper towels.
• Place something heavy on the tofu like a cold drink can or heavy pan.
• Let the moisture drain out from the tofu for 20-25 minutes.
• You can serve the remaining portion to your family. Season with salt and pepper before serving.
• You can store leftovers in an airtight container in the refrigerator. It can last for a week. Reheat in a pan to serve.

Tomato Red Lentil Stew

Ingredients:

1 small onion, minced
¾ cup red lentils, rinsed
½ cup canned or crushed tomatoes or tomato sauce
2.5 ounces fresh baby spinach
Freshly ground pepper to taste
½ tablespoon olive oil
2 ¼ cups vegetable broth or water
½ cup cherry tomatoes
A pinch freshly ground pepper

Directions:

Step 1: Place a heavy saucepan (that has a fitting lid) over medium heat.
Step 2: Pour oil into the saucepan and allow it to heat.
Step 3: When the oil is hot, add onion and cook until translucent.
Step 4: Add lentils and broth and wait for it to start boiling.
Step 5: Place the lid on the saucepan and lower the heat. Cook until the lentils are tender.
Step 6: Stir in crushed tomatoes and heat thoroughly.
Step 7: Stir in cherry tomatoes and baby spinach.
Step 8: Once the spinach wilts, turn off the heat.
Step 9: Add a pinch of pepper and serve to your baby.

Notes:

• If you have time on hand, you can soak the lentils for about two hours; this makes cooking quicker.
• You can serve this dish over cooked rice or with bread.
• You can slightly blend the stew for your baby if desired.
• Once you are done with your baby's meal, add salt, pepper, and chili flakes, and mix well. • You can now enjoy it with your family, served over rice or with crusty bread.

Moroccan Stew

Ingredients:
1 ½ tablespoons canola or olive oil
1 clove garlic, peeled and crushed
1 ½ tablespoons tomato puree
2 cups homemade vegetable stock
1 teaspoon ground coriander
1 teaspoon ground cumin
½ teaspoon turmeric powder
1 teaspoon ground cinnamon
A pinch black pepper
1 large carrot, peeled and cubed
1 small zucchini, trimmed and cubed
1 large sweet potato, peeled and cubed
1 bell pepper, diced
A handful kale leaves (optional)
1 small white onion, minced
1 can (14.5 ounces) chickpeas (or use cooked chickpeas)
1 inch piece fresh ginger, peeled and grated
1 can (14.5 ounces) chopped tomatoes
Coconut yogurt or soy yogurt to garnish

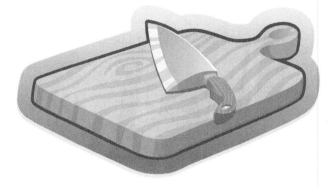

Directions:
Step 1: Pour oil into a soup pot and let it heat over medium heat.
Step 2: Once oil is hot, add onion and cook until onion turns translucent.
Step 3: Stir in ginger and garlic and cook for about a minute, or until you get a nice aroma.
Step 4: Add tomatoes, tomato puree, and spices and mix until well incorporated.
Step 5: Add stock, vegetables, and chickpeas, and stir.
Step 6: When the mixture starts boiling, lower the heat and cook until the sweet potatoes are soft.
Step 7: Stir in thyme and kale and cook until kale wilts. Turn off the heat.
Step 8: Serve stew in a bowl for your baby. Mash the chickpeas with the back of the spoon, just in case you are worried about choking.
Step 9: Add salt to the rest of the stew and enjoy it with your family.

Chapter

09

MEAT DINNER RECIPES

 Makes: 8-10 baby servings
Age: 6 months +

Beef Tagine

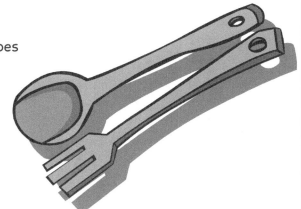

Ingredients:
2 teaspoons oil
½ red bell pepper, diced
1 small sweet potato, peeled and diced
1 can (28 ounces) unsalted chopped tomatoes
(or fresh tomatoes)
6 tablespoons apple juice
1 medium onion, chopped
2 small zucchinis, diced
7 ounces lean minced beef
2 medium carrots, peeled and diced
1 teaspoon ground cumin
1 cup water

Directions:
Step 1: Pour oil into a saucepan and let it heat over medium heat.
Step 2: Add bell pepper, sweet potato, onion, zucchini, and carrot and stir-fry for about four minutes.
Step 3: Stir the beef into the vegetable mixture. Cook until the beef is brown.
Step 4: Add cumin and mix well, stirring often.
Step 5: Add water, tomatoes, and apple juice, and stir well.
Step 6: When the mixture starts boiling, lower the heat and cook until the meat is tender.
Step 7: Turn off the heat.
Step 8: Take out the portion of tagine for your baby and blend to the desired texture to serve.
Step 9: To the remaining tagine, add salt and pepper and any other seasonings of your choice to taste and enjoy it with your family.
Step 10: Store leftover tagine in an airtight container in the refrigerator. It can last for five days.

Salmon and Corn
Chowder

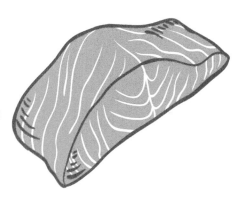

Ingredients:

1 medium potato, peeled and cubed
1 carrot, peeled and cubed
½ large onion, chopped
½ can (from a 16.5 ounces can) cream-style corn
½ cup chopped celery
1 cup chicken broth (or water)
2 small cloves garlic, peeled and minced
1 teaspoon olive oil
½ can (from a 16 ounce can) flaked salmon, drained
½ cup milk
¼ teaspoon dried marjoram (optional)

Directions:

Step 1: Pour oil into a saucepan and let it heat over medium heat.
Step 2: Once oil is hot, add onion, carrot, potato, and celery, and stir.
Step 3: Reduce the heat to low and cook for about 10 minutes.
Step 4: Stir in the garlic and cook for a few minutes, until you get a nice aroma.
Step 5: Stir in the water or broth and cook until the vegetables are soft.
Step 6: Stir in the salmon, milk, and corn.
Step 7: Raise the heat. When the mixture begins to boil, lower the heat once again and let it simmer for a couple of minutes.
Step 8: Turn off the heat.
Step 9: Take out the required portion for your baby and blend to the desired consistency. (For older babies, do not blend; you can mash it up a bit.)
Step 10: To the remaining chowder, add salt and pepper to taste. Enjoy it with your family.

Baby Burgers

Ingredients:

½ pound ground beef (or veal)

¼ cup diced onion

½ apple, peeled, cored, and grated

¼ teaspoon pepper to taste (optional)

¼ teaspoon dried sage (optional)

Directions:

Step 1: Preheat the oven to 400°F.

Step 2: Prepare a baking sheet by lining it with parchment paper.

Step 3: Combine meat, onion, pepper, apple, and sage in a bowl.

Step 4: Make 6-7 equal portions of the mixture and shape them into burgers about ¾ inch thick.

Step 5: Place the burgers on the baking sheet. Put the baking sheet in the oven and set the timer for about 20 minutes. Flip the burgers after about 12-15 minutes of baking.

Step 6: Serve warm to your baby. You can cut into strips for your baby to hold it easily.

Step7: Store the leftover burgers in an airtight container in the refrigerator. It can last for five days.

Makes: 2-3 baby servings
Age: 6 months +

Turkey, Squash, Carrot, and Kale

Ingredients:
1 teaspoon olive or sunflower oil
1 small carrot, diced
1 leek, diced
A handful kale leaves
¼ cup grated cheddar cheese
five ounces butternut squash, peeled, deseeded, and diced
¾ cup unsalted or very low-sodium chicken stock
five ounces cooked turkey, diced

Directions:
Step 1: Pour the oil into a pan and let it heat over medium heat.
Step 2: Add squash, carrot, and leek, and sauté for a couple of minutes.
Step 3: Stir in the stock.
Step 4: Cook covered on low heat until the vegetables are fork tender.
Step 5: Stir in the kale and cook for a few minutes, or until the kale wilts.
Step 6: Stir in the turkey, and turn off the heat.
Step 7: Blend the mixture with an immersion blender until the texture you desire is achieved. (As your baby grows, keep it chunkier.)

Makes: 18-20 bites
Age: 7 months +

Fish Pie Bites

Ingredients:

2 medium russet potatoes
⅛ cup frozen corn kernels, thawed
⅛ cup frozen peas, thawed
1.75 ounces mild cheddar cheese, grated
2 small salmon filets (4 ounces each)
2 teaspoons chopped chives
1 small egg, beaten

Directions:

Step 1: Preheat the oven to 350°F.

Step 2: Prepare a baking sheet by lining it with parchment paper.

Step 3: Take two sheets of foil and place a potato on each. Wrap them up and place them on the baking sheet.

Step 4: Place the baking sheet in the oven and set the timer for 75 minutes.

Step 5: Take another sheet of foil, and place the fish filets on it. Wrap them up and place them along with the potatoes. Bake for about 12 minutes, or until the fish flakes easily when you pierce it with a fork.

Step 6: If the fish is cooked, take it out. Check if the potatoes are cooked. If not, cook them for a bit longer.

Step 7: Take out the potatoes and unwrap the potatoes and fish. Let them cool for a few minutes, until you are able to handle them.

Step 8: Grease a baking sheet with some cooking spray.

Step 9: Discard the skin and bones from the fish, and flake it.

Step 10: Place the fish flakes into a bowl.

Step 11: Peel the potatoes and mash them up.

Step 12: Place the potato mash into the bowl of fish flakes.

Step 13: Add chives, egg, corn, and peas, and mix well. (You can slightly crush the corn and peas in a blender, if desired.)

Step 14: Make 18–20 equal portions of the mixture, and form the portions into oval-shaped bites.

Step 15: Place the bites on the baking sheet.

Step 16: Place the baking sheet in the refrigerator for 30 to 40 minutes.

Step 17: Increase the temperature of the oven to 400°F.

Step 18: Bake the bites for 15–20 minutes, until golden brown on the outside.

Step 19: Cool for at least 10 minutes before serving.

Notes:

• You can freeze these for future use. Make sure to thaw them completely before cooking.

• You can make the required quantity for your baby and add some salt to the rest of the mixture for you and your family.

Apricot Chicken and Rice

Ingredients:
2 teaspoons olive oil
4 dried apricots, chopped into small pieces
2 small plum tomatoes, deseeded, and diced
½ teaspoon chopped fresh rosemary
⅛ teaspoon ground cinnamon
⅛ teaspoon ground coriander
⅛ teaspoon minced garlic
2 tablespoons basmati rice, rinsed
½ small onion, diced
2 tablespoons chicken breast or thigh, cooked or raw
4 teaspoons sultanas
¾ cup water

Directions:
Step 1: Chop the sultanas into smaller pieces if desired.
Step 2: Pour the oil into a saucepan and let it heat over medium heat.
Step 3: Once the oil is hot, add the onion and cook until pink.
Step 4: Stir in the chicken, garlic, coriander, cinnamon, rosemary, apricot, sultanas, tomatoes, and water.
Step 5: Lower the heat and cook covered for about 15 minutes., stirring occasionally.
Step 6: Cook the rice following the instructions given on the package.
Step 7: Put half of the rice into a bowl.
Step 8: Add half of the chicken mixture and mix well. (Mash as you mix if you are just introducing this recipe to your baby. Add a little water to get the desired consistency if desired.)
Step 9: You can serve the remaining half of the rice and chicken to any other kid at home, eat it up yourself, or store in separate airtight containers in the refrigerator.

Notes:
• You can use leftover rice or any rice that is cooked for your family.
• Do not store the chicken and rice in the same container.
• Eat within four days.

130

Makes: 15-16 fingers
Age: 7 months +

Broccoli, Chicken, and Potato Fingers

Ingredients:
5.3 ounces broccoli florets
1.8 ounces grated parmesan cheese
2.8 ounces dried panko or regular breadcrumbs
4 spring onions, thinly sliced
7.8 ounces cooked potatoes, mashed, and cooled
4.2 ounces cooked and diced chicken
2 eggs, beaten
4 tablespoons sunflower or olive oil

Directions:
Step 1: Steam the broccoli for six minutes, or until tender.
Step 2: Let the broccoli cool completely.
Step 3: Finely chop the broccoli and place into a bowl.
Step 4: Add the potato, cheese, spring onions, chicken, one egg, and half of the breadcrumbs into the bowl of broccoli and mix well.
Step 5: Divide the mixture into 15-16 equal portions and shape into sticks the size of fingers. (Your baby should be able to hold it in their hand.)
Step 6: Place the sticks on a plate.
Step 7: Prepare a tray by lining it with parchment paper.
Step 8: It is now time to set up the breading ingredients. Place the remaining breadcrumbs on a plate.
Step 9: Place the remaining beaten egg beside the plate. Keep the prepared tray next to it.
Step 10: First dip the fingers in the egg, one at a time.
Step 11: Shaking off excess egg, dredge the fingers in breadcrumbs, and place them on the tray.
Step 12: Place the tray in the refrigerator for 30 to 40 minutes.
Step 13: Place a pan over medium heat. Pour half the oil into it, and let it heat.
Step 14: When the oil is hot, place 7-8 fingers in the pan.
Step 15: Cook until golden brown all over, turning occasionally.
Step 16: Remove the fingers with a slotted spoon, and place them on a plate lined with paper towels. Serve.

Notes:
• If you want to serve fingers for the rest of your family, take out as many as required for your baby, and add salt to taste to the remaining mixture, before shaping them.
• You can store the breaded fingers in an airtight container in the refrigerator and fry it for your baby later. Use it up within five days.

Mexican Mince and Rice

Ingredients:
1 tablespoon olive oil
8.8 ounces beef, lamb, or pork mince
1 teaspoon dried oregano
5.5-6 ounces fresh or frozen spinach
½ cup water
½ cup fresh or frozen corn kernels
½ large onion, finely chopped
1 tablespoon ground cumin
½ teaspoon garlic powder
1 medium carrot, peeled, and diced
½ cup rice, rinsed well
1 can (14.1 ounces) unsalted tomatoes
1 tablespoon paprika (optional)
¼ teaspoon red chili flakes (optional)

Directions:
Step 1: Add oil to a Dutch oven, or heavy-bottomed saucepan with a fitting lid, and warm over medium heat.
Step 2: Once the oil is hot, add the carrot and onion, and sauté until slightly light brown.
Step 3: Stir in the meat and spices.
Step 4: Cook until the meat is brown, stirring frequently.
Step 5: Meanwhile, pour half of the tomatoes and the spinach into a blender, and blend the mixture until smooth.
Step 6: Pour the blended mixture into the meat mixture.
Step 7: Add the remaining tomatoes, rice, and water, and mix well.
Step 8: Keep the pot covered and cook on low heat for about 12-15 minutes.
Step 9: Stir in corn.
Step 10: Cook until the mixture is dry and the rice is cooked. (If the rice is not cooked, add more water or stock and cook until the rice is tender.)
Step 11: Take out the required portion for your baby, and mash it up if desired.
Step 12: To the rest of the dish, add salt, some red chili flakes, and paprika and mix well.

Notes:
• You can use any other Mexican seasonings of your choice.

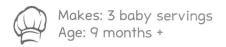

Makes: 3 baby servings
Age: 9 months +

Baked
Chicken Tenders

Ingredients:
¼ pound chicken tenders
¼ teaspoon garlic powder
¼ teaspoon paprika
⅛ teaspoon onion powder
Roasted Sweet Potatoes*

Directions:
Step 1: Preheat your oven to 450°F.
Step 2: Prepare a baking sheet by greasing it with some cooking spray. (You can also place a sheet of parchment paper or aluminum foil.)
Step 3: Place the chicken tenders in a bowl.
Step 4: Drizzle oil over the chicken, and sprinkle the garlic powder, paprika and onion powder on top.
Step 5: Toss well.
Step 6: Spread the chicken evenly across the baking sheet.
Step 7: Bake until well-cooked inside, about 20 minutes.
Step 8: Take out the chicken from the oven and place on your cutting board. Cut the chicken or shred the chicken into smaller pieces depending on the preference of your baby.
Step 9: Serve with roasted sweet potatoes.

*Notes:
• You can swap these spices for any other spices of your choice.
• The Roasted Sweet Potatoes recipe is in "Part 2: Lunch Recipes."

Kale Pesto Chicken Quesadilla

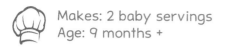

Makes: 2 baby servings
Age: 9 months +

Ingredients:

For quesadilla:
1 small whole-wheat tortilla
3-4 tablespoons cooked and finely chopped or shredded chicken
½ - 1 tablespoon kale pesto
⅛ cup shredded mozzarella cheese

For kale pesto:
½ cup packed basil
½ cup packed kale
1 teaspoon lemon juice
¼ cup parmesan cheese
1 clove garlic, peeled
¼ cup olive oil
Salt and pepper to taste (optional)

Directions:
Step 1: Spread the pesto* on the tortilla.
Step 2: Heat a pan over medium heat and.
Step 3: Place the tortilla on the pan, pesto side up.
Step 4: Scatter the chicken on one half of the tortilla.
Step 5: Sprinkle cheese over the chicken.
Step 6: Fold the other half of the tortilla over the filling and press lightly.
Step 7: When the underside is golden brown, turn the quesadilla over and cook the other side until golden brown.
Step 8: Remove the quesadilla from the pan and let it cool.
Step 9: Cut into four wedges to serve.

*Notes:
• You can make your own pesto or use store-bought one.
• To make your own pesto, place basil, kale, lemon juice, cheese, garlic, and oil in a blender and blend until smooth.
• Use as much as required and store the remaining in an airtight container in the refrigerator.
• Use it within five days.
• You can make quesadillas for your family as well. Make sure to add some salt and pepper to the pesto for you and your family.

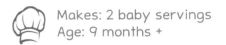
Chicken
and Pea Carbonara

Ingredients:

3.5 ounces small-size pasta
¼ cup full-fat milk
1 ounce parmesan cheese, grated
1 ounce ripe avocado, diced
1.8 ounces peas, fresh or frozen
2 egg yolks
1.8 ounces cooked chicken, diced

Directions:

Step 1: Cook the pasta, following the directions given on the package.

Step 2: Drop the peas into the boiling pasta during the last three minutes of cooking.

Step 3: Drain the pasta in a colander.

Step 4: Add the drained pasta back into the saucepan it was cooked in.

Step 5: Combine yolks, milk, and cheese in a bowl.

Step 6: Whisk well and pour the mixture into the saucepan with the pasta.

Step 7: Place the saucepan over low heat and stir until the sauce is thick.

Step 8: Turn off the heat.

Step 9: Add the chicken and avocado, and serve. Once you serve your baby, enjoy the remaining yourself by adding some seasonings of your choice.

Beef Casserole for Babies

Ingredients:

2.6 ounces beef kidney, halved, white parts removed, and cut into small bite-size pieces
7 ounces beef steak, trimmed of fat, and cut into about ¾-inch chunks
½ onion, finely chopped
1 ½ teaspoons cooking oil
1 carrot, peeled and chopped
1 stick celery, chopped
1 medium potato, peeled, and chopped
1 small orange sweet potato, peeled and chopped
1 teaspoon minced fresh thyme
1 tablespoon minced fresh parsley
1 ½ tablespoons Worcestershire sauce
1 cup low-salt or unsalted beef stock (or water)
1 ½ teaspoons flour (or cornstarch)
½ teaspoon paprika (optional)
2 small cloves garlic, peeled, and minced (optional)

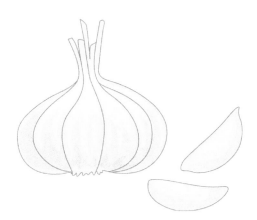

Directions:

Step 1: Preheat the oven to 330°F.
Step 2: Heat the oil in a stovetop casserole dish over medium heat.
Step 3: When the oil is hot, add the garlic and onion and cook until soft.
Step 4: Stir in all of the vegetables and cook for a few minutes,
Step 5: Stir in the meat, stock, and thyme.
Step 6: Turn off the heat.
Step 7: Cover the casserole dish and place into the oven. Cook for about 1 ½ - 2 hours, or until meat is cooked.
Step 8: Remove the dish from the oven and take out the required portion for your baby. Let it cool completely. Blend the mixture to the texture your baby prefers or chop the meat into small pieces.
Step 9: To the remaining stew add Worcestershire sauce, salt, and pepper to taste.
Step 10: Place the casserole dish back over medium heat.
Step 11: Whisk together cornstarch or flour with a tablespoon or two of water, and pour into the casserole dish.
Step 12: Stir constantly until thick.
Step 13: Serve the casserole to the rest of your family.

Notes:

• Store leftovers in an airtight container in the refrigerator. Use within four days.

Makes: 12 baby servings
Age: 9 months +

Baby Taco

Ingredients:
2 tablespoons olive oil
1 cup canned or cooked black beans, rinsed
1 pound lean ground turkey
4 teaspoons chili powder (or to taste)
1 teaspoon garlic powder
2 teaspoons paprika or to taste
½ teaspoon onion powder
⅔ cup shredded cheese
¼ cup water

To serve:
1 avocado, peeled, pitted, and chopped
1 tomato, chopped
1 red bell pepper, deseeded, and chopped

Directions:
Step 1: Pour oil into a large pan.
Step 2: Place the pan over medium heat. When oil is hot, add turkey and stir.
Step 3: As you stir, break the turkey into smaller pieces and cook until they are brown.
Step 4: Stir in the beans, water, and all of the spices. Add only a little of the chili powder and paprika.
Step 5: Lower the heat and cook on low for about five minutes, stirring often.
Step 6: Remove from heat and let it cool.
Step 7: Serve the required baby portion on a plate. (You can mash up the beans slightly if desired.)
Step 8: Garnish with cheese and serve topped with a little (about a teaspoon) of each: avocado, tomato, and pepper.
Step 9: To the remaining taco filling, add the remaining chili powder, paprika and some salt to taste. Serve it over tortillas with suggested toppings, to you and your family.

Notes:
• Store leftovers in an airtight container in the refrigerator. Use within four days.
• Make sure to chop the avocado, pepper, and tomato fresh, on the day of serving.

Makes: 1-2 baby servings
Age: 9 months +

Bolognese for Babies

Ingredients:

¼ teaspoon olive oil

½ clove garlic, peeled, minced

½ small carrot, peeled, finely chopped

½ can (from a 28 ounces can) crushed tomatoes

½ teaspoon dried parsley

⅛ teaspoon dried oregano

¼ teaspoon dried basil

¼ cup diced onions

¼ pound ground turkey or chicken or beef or pork

3 tablespoons finely chopped zucchini

½ tablespoon tomato paste

Cooked pasta of your choice to serve

Directions:

Step 1: Pour oil into a skillet and place the saucepan over medium heat. Once oil is hot, add onion and garlic and cook until soft.

Step 2: Stir in the meat and cook until brown. As you stir, break the meat into smaller pieces. Discard any extra cooked fat from the pan.

Step 3: Mix in carrot and zucchini and cook for a couple of minutes.

Step 4: Stir in tomato paste, canned tomatoes, and dried herbs. When the mixture begins to boil, lower the heat and cook for about 10 minutes. Make sure to stir occasionally.

Step 5: Take out the required portion for your baby and serve it over cooked pasta. For a start you can slightly blend the pasta into smaller pieces. You can add salt to the remaining sauce and use it for your family dinner. If there is any remaining sauce, cool completely and transfer it into an airtight container in the refrigerator. Use within five days.

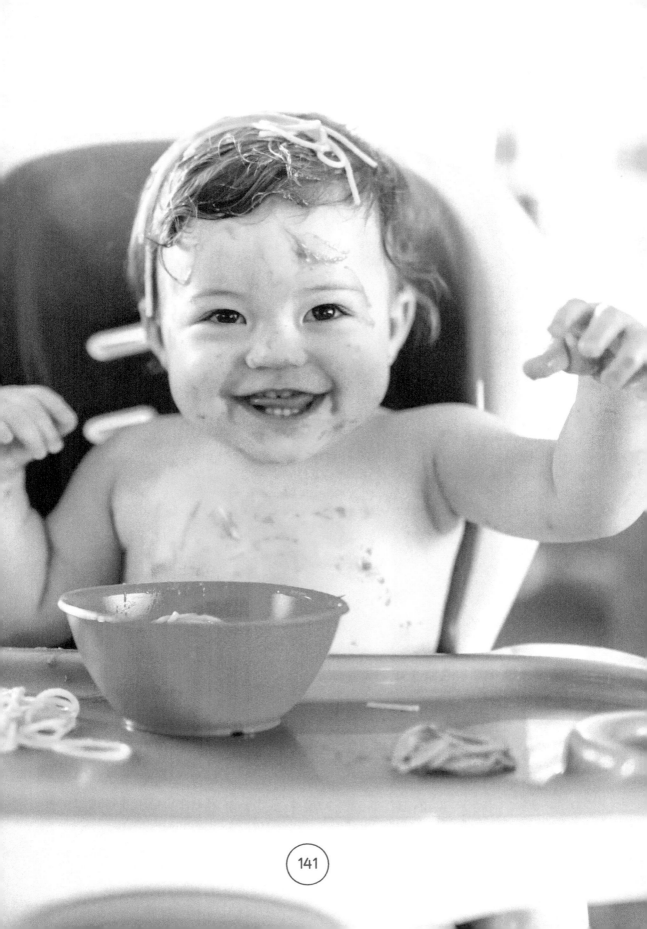

Asian Turkey Rice Meatballs

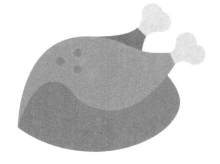

Ingredients:

½ pound lean ground turkey
1 ½ teaspoons sesame oil
¼ teaspoon garlic powder
6 tablespoons cooked rice
6 tablespoons finely chopped mixed vegetables of your choice
⅛ cup shredded cheese (optional)

Directions:

Step 1: Preheat the oven to 350°F.
Step 2: Prepare a baking sheet by lining it with parchment paper.
Step 3: Pour ½ teaspoon of the oil into a skillet and let it heat over medium-high heat.
Step 4: Once the oil is hot, add the mixed vegetables and cook until they are tender.
Step 5: Turn off the heat and put the vegetables into a bowl.
Step 6: Add the rice, garlic, powder, 1 teaspoon sesame oil, and cheese into the bowl of vegetables.
Step 7: Mix with your hands, making sure not to over mix, or else the meat will become tough.
Step 8: Dip your hands in water and make small meatballs of the mixture. Place them on the prepared baking sheet. (Once the meat starts sticking to your hand, dip your hands again in water.)
Step 9: Pour some water into a small baking dish and place it on the baking sheet along with the meatballs.
Step 10: Bake for 20 minutes. Turn the meatballs after 12 minutes of baking.
Step 11: Serve your baby. The rest can be served to your family.

Notes:

• Preferably use soft cooked rice. If the rice is not soft, place it in a microwave-safe bowl. • Add about four tablespoons of water and cook on High until soft and dry.
• You can store the leftover meatballs in an airtight container in the refrigerator. Make sure to use it up within five days.

Chapter

10

SNACKS

Tropical Treat

Ingredients:

⅛ cup diced ripe peeled avocado

⅛ cup diced peeled papaya

¼ small banana, sliced

¼ kiwi, peeled, sliced

⅛ cup plain natural yogurt

2 drops maple syrup (optional)

Directions:

Step 1: Place the fruits in a bowl.

Step 2: Add yogurt (and maple syrup if using) and mix well.

Step 3: Serve.

Notes:

• For the first time when you introduce this recipe to a 6 months old baby, blend the fruits to the texture you desire.

• For older babies, 9 months and above, do not puree the fruits.

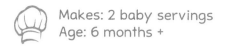

Makes: 2 baby servings
Age: 6 months +

Egg Pudding

Ingredients:

2 eggs
½ cup milk
4 drops vanilla extract (optional)
⅛ teaspoon ground cinnamon (optional)

Directions:

Step 1: Crack the eggs into a bowl and beat with a fork.

Step 2: Beat in the milk.

Step 3: Add vanilla extract and cinnamon if using, and whisk well.

Step 4: Pour the mixture into two ramekins.

Step 5: Steam for 20 minutes.

Step 6: Remove from the steamer and cool until warm.

Step 7: Serve.

Notes:

• You can store the other pudding in the refrigerator. Use it within five days.

145

Makes: 10-12 small fritters
Age: 6 months +

Banana and Blueberry
Fritters

Ingredients:

4 ripe bananas, peeled and mashed

½ cup blueberries

2 teaspoons coconut oil (or more if required)

½ – 1 cup buckwheat flour (or plain flour)

½ teaspoon ground cinnamon (optional)

Directions:

Step 1: Mix mashed banana, cinnamon, and blueberries in a bowl.

Step 2: Add about ½ cup of flour and mix well. (If the mixture is very runny and the fritters are getting disintegrated, add some more flour, a tablespoon at a time and mix well each time.)

Step 3: Place a non-stick pan over high heat. Add a teaspoon of oil and wait for it to melt. Step 4: Swirl the pan to spread the oil.

Step 5: Take a tablespoonful of batter and drop it in the pan. Place as many as can fit in the pan.

Step 6: Cook until the underside is golden brown. Turn the fritters over and cook the other side until golden brown.

Step 7: Transfer the fritters onto a plate.

Step 8: Make the remaining fritters similarly, adding more oil in each batch.

Step 9: Serve warm. Once you serve your baby, you can enjoy the fritters along with your family.

Three-flavored Popsicles

Ingredients:

Mango and Carrot Popsicles:
¼ cup finely diced ripe mango
½ cup apple juice
1 medium carrot, peeled and grated

Strawberry Popsicle:
3.5 ounces chopped strawberries
2 tablespoons apple juice
2 tablespoons plain yogurt

Blueberry and Banana Popsicle:
½ banana, sliced
⅓ cup apple juice
⅓ cup blueberries
2 tablespoons plain yogurt

Directions:
Step 1: Place the chosen combination ingredients in a blender and blend until the texture you desire is achieved.
Step 2: Pour into two baby popsicle molds. Insert popsicle sticks and freeze until firm.
Step 3: Remove from the mold and give it to your baby in his/her hand to enjoy.

Notes:
• When you serve it to your baby, dip the popsicle mold in a bowl of warm water for 10 to 15 seconds. The popsicle will loosen up.
• You can also make all the popsicles using a different combination and can give a different flavor to your baby daily.

Banana Muffins

Ingredients:
2 cups mashed overripe banana
½ cup melted coconut oil, a bit cooled
2 teaspoons vanilla extract
2 large eggs
2 cups milk of your choice
2 cups whole-wheat flour
2 teaspoons ground cinnamon
1 teaspoon baking soda
2 teaspoons baking powder
1 ½ cups rolled oats
A pinch salt

Directions:
Step 1: Preheat the oven to 375°F.
Step 2: Prepare two muffin pans of 12 counts each by spraying them with cooking spray. (Place disposable paper liners in the muffin cups if desired.)
Step 3: Combine flour, oats, baking soda, cinnamon, salt, and baking powder in a bowl.
Step 4: Whisk oil, banana, eggs, vanilla, and milk in another large mixing bowl.
Step 5: Add the mixture of dry ingredients into the bowl of wet ingredients and mix until well incorporated, making sure not to over beat.
Step 6: Pour equal quantity of batter into the muffin cups. Each cup should fill up to about ⅔ full.
Step 7: Bake for 15 minutes.
Step 8: Chop up a muffin into bite size chunks and serve to your baby. The remaining muffins can be enjoyed by you and your family.

Notes:
• You can also make mini-muffins in mini-muffin pans.
• You can check if the muffins are done by inserting a toothpick in the center of the muffin. Take out the toothpick and check if you can see any particles stuck on the toothpick. If you find particles, you need to bake for a few more minutes.
• Store leftover muffins in an airtight container in the refrigerator. They last for about seven days.

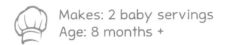

Makes: 2 baby servings
Age: 8 months +

Baby Guacamole

Ingredients:

½ ripe avocado, peeled, pitted, and mashed
½ teaspoon minced fresh cilantro
½ tablespoon tomato juice
A pinch ground cumin
Carrot sticks (to serve)

Directions:

Step 1: Mix avocado, cilantro, cumin, and tomato juice in a bowl until smooth.
Step 2: Serve your baby with carrot sticks.

Makes: 12-15 bites
Age: 9 months +

Crispy Herb Salmon Bites

Ingredients:

1 pound salmon filets, skinless, cut into 1-inch thick pieces
4 large eggs, beaten
2 tablespoons Italian seasoning
½ cup white whole-wheat flour
2 cups panko breadcrumbs
6 teaspoons dried parsley
Pepper to taste (optional)

Directions:

Step 1: Preheat the oven to 450°F.

Step 2: Prepare a baking sheet by lining it with parchment paper.

Step 3: Dry the salmon by patting it with paper towels.

Step 4: Combine the flour and pepper (if using) in a shallow bowl.

Step 5: Combine the breadcrumbs, Italian seasoning, parsley, and pepper (if using) in another shallow bowl.

Step 6: Working with one piece of salmon at a time, dredge the salmon in the bowl of flour.

Step 7: Shake off excess flour and dip in the egg.

Step 8: Shaking off the excess egg, dredge in breadcrumbs.

Step 9: Press well to adhere and place on the baking sheet.

Step 10: When you are done with the required number of pieces for your baby, add salt to taste to the bowl of flour as well as to the bowl of breadcrumbs. This is for your family members.

Step 11: Place the baking sheet in the oven and set the timer for 20 minutes, or until crisp on the outside and cooked through inside.

Step 12: Serve once it cools a bit.

Makes: 6-8 muffins
Age: 9 months +

Veggie and Sesame Seed Muffins

Ingredients:
½ carrot, peeled and grated
½ medium zucchini, grated
⅛ cup frozen corn kernels
⅛ cup frozen peas
2 cup whole-wheat flour
¼ cup grated cheddar cheese
⅛ cup plain Greek yogurt
1 egg
1 teaspoon mixed herbs
¼ cup whole cow milk
⅛ cup canola oil
1 ½ teaspoons baking powder
1 teaspoon sesame seeds

Directions:
Step 1: Preheat the oven to 350°F.
Step 2: Prepare a 12-count muffin pan by spraying it with cooking spray.
Step 3: Combine the flour and baking powder in a bowl.
Step 4: Mix the vegetables, herbs, milk, cheese, egg, sesame seeds, and oil in another bowl.
Step 5: Add the flour mixture to the vegetable mix, and mix until well combined.
Step 6: Divide the batter among the muffin cups. Fill the cups half-full.
Step 7: Bake for 25 minutes or until firm to the touch and slightly brown on top.
Step 8: Place the muffin pan on a wire rack. Run a knife around the edges of the muffins to loosen it.
Step 9: Chop up a muffin into bite size chunks for your baby and serve with hummus or guacamole (or any vegetable puree if desired).
Step 10: Serve the rest of the muffins to your family with a dip of your choice.
Step 11: Store leftover muffins in an airtight container in the refrigerator. They can last for about seven days. Warm them up slightly before serving.

Makes: 6-8 biscuits
Age: 9 months +

Teething Biscuits

Ingredients:

1 cup dry oats
1 tablespoon coconut oil
½ medium ripe banana, sliced
A pinch ground cinnamon (optional)
½ teaspoon vanilla extract (optional)

Directions:

Step 1: Preheat the oven to 350°F.

Step 2: Line a baking sheet with parchment paper.

Step 3: Place the oats in a blender or food processor and process until finely powdered.

Step 4: Place the banana, vanilla, cinnamon, and oil into the blender with oats and blend until well combined.

Step 5: Transfer the mixture into a bowl.

Step 6: Make eight equal portions of the mixture and shape into bars of about ½ inch thick, 4 inches in length, and 1 ½ inches in width.

Step 7: Once the bars are made, make sure to pat the edges until slightly rounded. This is necessary so that the baby does not get hurt with the edges if the edges are sharp.

Step 8: Place the bars on the baking sheet, leaving sufficient space between them.

Step 9: Bake for 10 minutes. Turn sides and continue baking for about 10 minutes or until golden brown around the edges. The centers should be set but not too firm or crunchy.

Notes:

• If the mixture is very moist and you are unable to shape into bars, add a little whole wheat flour or gluten-free flour.

• If the mixture is very dry, add some more coconut oil and mix well.

Makes: 1 baby serving
Age: 7 months +

Egg Roll-Up

Ingredients:

1 large egg
½ tablespoon milk
½ tablespoon butter or oil
1 tablespoon shredded cheddar cheese (optional)

Directions:

Step 1: Melt butter in a non-stick pan over medium heat.

Step 2: Whisk egg and milk together in a bowl.

Step 3: Pour egg mixture into the heated pan.

Step 4: Cook for about a minute, and then scatter the cheese on top.

Step 5: Place a lid on the pan and cook for a couple of minutes until the egg is set.

Step 6: Carefully slide the egg onto a plate.

Step 7: Roll the egg starting from one side, right up to the opposite side, and place it with the seam side facing down. Let it cool for a few minutes

Step 8: Cut into two halves. Make your baby hold one piece and let him/her enjoy it. You can feed them the other half in between bites.

Chapter

11

SAVORY FROZEN
RECIPES

Butternut Squash and Goat Cheese
Pancakes

Makes: 10-12 baby pancakes
Age: 7 months +

Ingredients:
½ cup plain or buckwheat flour
½ cup whole milk
1 tablespoon unsalted butter, melted (+ extra to cook)
1 ½ tablespoons goat cheese
½ egg
1 teaspoon baking powder
½ cup pureed, roasted butternut squash
½ teaspoon finely chopped fresh rosemary

Directions:
Step 1: Combine flour and baking powder in a bowl.
Step 2: Add egg, milk, and butter into another bowl and whisk until well combined.
Step 3: Make a depression in the center of the flour and pour the milk mixture into the depression. Whisk until smooth.
Step 4: Whisk in butternut squash puree, rosemary, and goat cheese.
Step 5: Place a large pan over medium heat. Add a little butter into the pan. When butter melts, swirl the pan to spread the butter. Pour about 1/8 cup batter into the pan to make one pancake. Make as many as can fit in the pan.
Step 6: Soon bubbles will be visible on top of the pancakes. Cook until the underside is golden brown. Turn the pancakes over and cook the other side as well. Remove pancakes and place on a baking sheet.
Step 7: Make pancakes until all of the batter is gone. You can serve the pancakes now.

To freeze: Let the pancakes cool to room temperature. Keep the pancakes in a pile, placing parchment paper between the pancakes.
• Place the pile of pancakes in a freezer-safe bag and place in the freezer. It can last for about three months.

To serve: You can heat it up in the toaster or in a microwave before serving.

Notes:
• To make it vegan, replace butter with oil or vegan butter. Replace milk with non-dairy milk. Omit the egg and goat cheese.

161

Salmon, Potato, and Parsley
Mash/Fish Cakes

Ingredients:

3.5 ounces salmon filet
½ cup finely chopped fresh parsley
2 small eggs
10.5 ounces potatoes, peeled and cut into fries
2 teaspoons flour
Oil to fry (as required)

Directions:

Step 1: Steam the salmon and potatoes for 15 minutes.
Step 2: Set aside a couple of potato slices and place the remaining in a blender.
Step 3: Remove skin from the salmon filet and place it in the blender.
Step 4: Add parsley and blend the contents until well combined. (Add a tablespoon or two of milk or water while blending if required for mash only.)
Step 5: Transfer the mixture into a bowl. If you want to serve it as a mash, it is ready to serve.

To make fish cakes:

Step 1: Drain off any liquid from the mash and place in a bowl. Mix in eggs and flour. You may not need all the flour. (You may need more flour if the mixture is very moist.)
Step 2: Place a non-stick pan over medium heat. Add 1-2 teaspoons of oil and let it heat.
Step 3: Swirl the pan to spread oil.
Step 4: Scoop out some of the mixture and place on the pan. Press with the back of the spoon to flatten. Place 2-3 more fish cakes on the pan. When the underside is golden brown, turn the fish cakes over and cook the other side as well.
Step 5: Remove the fish cakes and place them on a baking sheet lined with parchment paper.
Step 6: Cook the remaining fish cakes similarly adding some oil in each batch.
Step 7: Place the baking sheet in the freezer and freeze until firm.
Step 8: Place the fritters in freezer bags and freeze until use. Use it up within two months.

Notes:

• To freeze mash: Place in a freezer-safe container and freeze until used. Make sure to use it within two months.

Vegetable Pancakes

Makes: 6 baby pancakes
Age: 9 months +

Ingredients:
½ cup plain or buckwheat flour
½ cup whole milk
1 tablespoon melted unsalted butter
½ small head broccoli, cut into florets
2 tablespoons grated cheddar cheese
1 teaspoon baking powder
½ egg
½ medium onion, chopped into chunks
½ red bell pepper, chopped into chunks
1 tablespoon olive oil (+ extra to fry pancakes)

To serve:
Sour cream
Finely chopped fresh herbs of your choice

Directions:
Step 1: Preheat the oven to 425°F.
Step 2: Place onion and bell pepper on a baking sheet and drizzle oil over the vegetables.
Step 3: Bake for about 25 minutes, until the vegetables are tender.
Step 4: Steam the broccoli for six minutes, or until tender.
Step 5: Let the roasted vegetables and broccoli cool for a few minutes.
Step 6: Chop the vegetables into very small pieces.
Step 7: Combine the flour and baking powder in a bowl.
Step 8: Add the egg, milk, and butter into another bowl, and whisk until well combined.
Step 9: Make a depression in the center of the flour and pour the milk mixture into the depression. Whisk until smooth.
Step 10: Add vegetables and cheese and fold gently. You will have thick batter.
Step 11: Place a large pan over medium heat. Add a little oil into the pan. Swirl the pan to spread the oil.
Step 12: Pour about a heaping tablespoon of the batter into the pan to make one pancake. Press the batter with the back of the spoon to flatten. Make as many as can fit in the pan.
Step 13: Soon bubbles will be visible on top of the pancakes. Cook until the underside is golden brown. Turn the pancakes over and cook the other side as well.
Step 14: Make pancakes until all of the batter is gone. You can serve the pancakes now.

To freeze: Let the pancakes cool to room temperature. Keep the pancakes in a pile, placing parchment paper between the pancakes. Place the pile of pancakes in a freezer-safe bag and place in the freezer. They last for about three months.

To serve: You can heat it up in the toaster or in a microwave before serving.

Notes:
To make it vegan, replace butter with oil or vegan butter. Replace milk with non-dairy milk.

Mini Quiches

Makes: 12 mini quiches
Age: 9 months +

Ingredients:
1 cup plain flour
1-2 tablespoons water
2.1 ounces butter
Canola oil or olive oil, as required
2 cloves garlic, peeled, minced
12 cherry tomatoes, quartered
2 eggs, well beaten
½ cup finely chopped spinach
6-7 fresh basil leaves, finely chopped
1.8 ounces grated cheddar cheese

Directions:
Step 1: Preheat the oven to 350°F.
Step 2: Add flour and butter into a mixing bowl. Cut the butter into the mixture with a pastry cutter until crumbly in texture.
Step 3: Add a tablespoon of water and mix well. Repeat this adding of water and mix well each time until you get dough.
Step 4: Dust your countertop with some flour.
Step 5: Place a dough ball on the countertop and roll the dough balls with a rolling pin until thin, approximately to a thickness of 0.2 inches.
Step 6: Take a cookie cutter and cut out 12 rounds from the rolled dough. (In case you do not have 12 rounds, collect the scrap dough and re-shape it into a ball.)
Step 7: Roll it once again and cut rounds from it. Repeat until you have 12 rounds.
Step 8: Take a mini-muffin pan of 12 counts and place a piece of cut dough in each muffin cup.
Step 9: Place the muffin pan in the refrigerator until your filling is ready.
Step 10: Pour the oil into a pan and let it heat over medium heat. Once oil is hot, add onions and cook until soft.
Step 11: Stir in garlic and cook for about a minute, until you get a nice aroma.
Step 12: Mix in the spinach and let it cook for a few minutes.
Step 13: Once spinach wilts, stir in tomatoes and basil and turn off the heat.
Step 14: Take out the muffin pan from the refrigerator. Divide the vegetable mixture among the muffin cups. You should be able to put in about ½ tablespoon of the filling in each cup.
Step 15: Drizzle the egg over the vegetables. Scatter cheese on top.
Step 16: Place the muffin pan in the oven and bake until the eggs are cooked.
Step 17: Cool to room temperature. Take out the quiche from the muffin pan and place in a freezer-safe container. Freeze until use. Make sure to use it within three months.
Step 18: Take out the required number of quiches. Thaw completely and heat in a microwave for a few seconds before serving. You can serve them cold as well.

Makes: 10-12 baby servings
Age: 7 months+

Irish Potato Cabbage and Carrot
Hash Browns

Ingredients:
4 medium potatoes, rinsed well, grated with skin
1 head cabbage, thinly shredded (about 4 large cups)
2 teaspoons onion powder
6-8 tablespoons canola oil
4 large carrots, peeled and grated
4 spring onions, thinly sliced
2 eggs, lightly beaten

To serve (for serving day):
Sour cream
Lemon juice
Minced fresh thyme leaves

Directions:
Step 1: Squeeze out as much moisture from the potatoes as possible.
Step 2: Place the potatoes in a bowl.
Step 3: Add cabbage, carrots, and spring onion into the bowl of potatoes and mix well.
Step 4: Stir in eggs and onion powder. Mix until well incorporated.
Step 5: Place a non-stick pan over medium heat. Add 1-2 tablespoons of oil. Scoop out some of the mixture and place on the pan. Flatten it to the shape of patties. Place as many as possible on the pan.
Step 6: Cook until the underside is light golden brown. Turn the hash browns over and cook the other side as well.
Step 7: Remove onto a baking sheet.
Step 8: Cook the remaining hash browns similarly, adding oil each time (steps 4-6).
Step 9: Place a layer of hash browns in a freezer-safe container, without overlapping. Place a sheet of parchment paper over the hash browns. Repeat this process until the hash browns are packed.
Step 10: Freeze until use.

To serve: Take out the required number of hash browns and thaw completely.
Reheat in a pan or in an oven.

To assemble: Place hash browns on serving plates. Drizzle some sour cream and lemon juice over the hash browns. Garnish with thyme and serve.

Beetroot, Kale, and Goat
Cheese Tart

Ingredients:

11.3 ounces plain flour

6-8 tablespoons water

2 cloves garlic, crushed

3.5 ounces kale leaves, chopped

7 ounces roasted beetroots, diced

5.6 ounces soft butter

2 small onions, finely chopped

2 sprigs fresh thyme, chopped (+ extra to garnish)

12 eggs, well beaten

6.3 ounces goat cheese

Directions:

Step 1: Preheat the oven to 350°F.

Step 2: To make pastry dough: Place flour in a bowl. Add butter and cut it into the flour with a pastry cutter until crumbly in texture. Add a tablespoon of water and mix well. Repeat this adding of water and mix well each time until you get dough.

Step 3: Dust your countertop with some flour.

Step 4: Divide the dough into two equal portions. Place a dough ball on the countertop and roll the dough balls with a rolling pin to a thickness of 0.2 inch.

Step 5: Grease 12 mini-tart pans with some butter.

Step 6: Cut out the dough into rounds that can fit into the mini-tart pans. Gather the scrap dough and re-roll once again. Cut out the dough again. Keep doing this until all the dough is used up. You should get approximately 12 tarts.

To make filling:

Step 1: Pour oil into a pan and let it heat over medium heat. When oil is hot, add onion and cook until onion turns translucent. Stir in garlic and cook for a couple of minutes.

Step 2: Stir in thyme and kale and cook for four minutes. Once kale wilts, turn off the heat and divide the mixture into the mini-tart pans.

Step 3: Pour egg over the vegetables in the tart pans.

Step 4: Divide the beetroot pieces among the tart pans.

Step 5: Pull off pieces of goat cheese and place in the pans in any visible gaps.

Step 6: Place as many as tart pans as can fit in the oven and set the timer for 30 minutes. Step 7: Bake until edges of the pastry turn golden brown and the center is firm.

Step 8: Serve as many as required and cool the others completely. Remove them from the pans and place on a baking sheet.

Step 9: Freeze until firm. Take them out and wrap each in cling wrap. Place them in freezer bags and freeze until use. They can last for three months.

To serve: Heat up the tarts in the microwave and serve.

Meatless Meatballs with Garlic Bread

Makes: 5 baby servings + 5 adult servings
Age: 10 months +

Ingredients:

For Meatless Meatballs:
½ cup olive oil
4 cloves garlic, peeled and crushed
4 sprigs fresh thyme leaves
2 handfuls fresh basil leaves
Pepper to taste
2 teaspoons English mustard
2 medium onions, roughly chopped
4 cans (14.5 ounces each) chickpeas, drained and rinsed
3 cups breadcrumbs
4 eggs

For garlic bread (on serving day):
4 tablespoons butter
4 sprigs fresh thyme leaves, minced
2 ciabatta loaves
4 cloves garlic, minced

For sauce (on serving day):
1 teaspoon olive oil
4 cloves garlic, peeled and thinly sliced
½ cup tomato puree
2 medium onions, finely chopped
2 cans (14.5 ounces each) chopped tomatoes
3 tablespoons apple cider vinegar

To garnish:
Grated parmesan cheese (optional)
Finely chopped fresh basil

Directions:

To make the meatballs:

Pour oil into a pan and let it heat over medium heat. When oil is hot, add onion and garlic and cook until onions turn pink.

Step 1: Turn off the heat and transfer the onion mixture into a food processor bowl.

Step 2: Add chickpeas, breadcrumbs, and herbs and process until chickpeas are chopped into smaller pieces and you are able to form into balls.

Step 3: Add eggs and give short pulses until well combined.

Step 4: Transfer the mixture into a bowl.

Step 5: Prepare a baking sheet by lining it with parchment paper.

Step 6: Make small meatballs of the mixture, about 1-1 ½ inches diameter and place on the baking sheet.

Step 7: Place the baking sheet in the freezer and freeze until firm.

Step 8: Remove the meatballs from the baking sheet and place in a freezer bag and freeze until use. They can last for three months.

Step 9: On the serving day, take out the meatballs and thaw them completely.

Step 10: Preheat the oven to 425°F.

Step 11: Prepare a baking sheet by lining it with parchment paper.

Step 12: Place the meatballs on the baking sheet and bake for 25 to 30 minutes, or until they are cooked and firm.

Step 13: Meanwhile, prepare the garlic bread. Combine butter, thyme, and garlic in a bowl.

Step 14: Place the bread loaves on a baking sheet. Smear the herb garlic butter over the bread loaves. Cover the baking sheet with foil.

Step 15: Place the baking sheet in the oven and set the timer for 15 minutes.

To make the sauce:

Step 1: Pour oil into a pan and let it heat over medium heat. Add onions and cook until onions turn pink.

Step 2: Stir in garlic and cook for a few seconds until you get a nice aroma.

Step 3: Stir in tomato puree, tomatoes, and vinegar and mix well. Cook on low until the sauce thickens slightly.

Step 4: Add the cooked meatballs into the sauce and mix well. Turn off the heat.

Step 5: Take out the required portion for your baby. Garnish with cheese and basil and serve to your baby with a slice of garlic bread.

Step 6: To the remaining meatballs and sauce, add salt and pepper to taste. You can add some red chili flakes as well. Mix well and serve garnished with cheese and basil for the rest of your family with garlic bread slices.

Chicken and Veggie Pot Pie

Makes: 2 family pies + 2 baby pies
Age: 10 months +

Ingredients:

For pastry:
2 pounds plain flour
1 cup water
1 pound butter

For filling:
2 tablespoons canola or olive oil
6 medium carrots, finely chopped
2 cloves garlic, crushed
4 packs tender stem broccoli spears, finely chopped
4 large mushrooms, finely chopped
4 medium onions, finely chopped
2 large handfuls fresh spinach, finely chopped
2 eggs, beaten
2 heaping tablespoons plain yogurt
8 chicken breasts, cut into small pieces
13.5 ounces whole milk
5.6 ounces parmesan cheese, grated
1 small bunch parsley, finely chopped
Pepper to taste
Water, as required

Directions:

Step 1: To make pastry dough: Place flour in a bowl. Add butter and cut it into the flour with a pastry cutter until crumbly in texture. Add a tablespoon of water and mix well. Repeat this adding of water and mix well each time until you get dough.

Step 2: Dust your countertop with some flour.

Step 3: Divide the dough into two equal portions. Place a dough ball on the countertop and roll the dough balls with a rolling pin to a thickness of 0.2 inch.

Step 4: Grease two pie pans and two ramekins with some butter. Cut out the rolled dough to fit into the pie pans and remove the excess dough.

Step 5: Gather the excess dough and shape it into a ball once again. Roll the dough once

again and cut the dough to fit into two ramekins. These are for your baby.

Step 6: Place the pie pans and ramekins in the refrigerator until the filling is made.

Step 7: Pour oil into a pan and place the pan over medium heat. Once oil is hot, add onion and carrots and cook until onions are pink.

Step 8: Stir in chicken and lower the heat. Once chicken is cooked, add garlic, yogurt, milk, and cheese and mix well. Turn off the heat.

Step 9: Stir in the chopped vegetables and parsley. Divide the filling among the pie pans and ramekins.

Step 10: Roll the other dough ball to a thickness of 0.2 inch. Cut out the dough to the size of the pans to cover the filling.

Step 11: Gather the scrap dough and re-roll the dough. Cut two rounds to fit the ramekins.

Step 12: Make a slit in each pie, on the top crust for the steam to escape.

Step 13: You can bake one pie pan and one ramekin for your baby and your family.

Step 14: Cover the other pie pan and ramekin with cling wrap and freeze until use. Make sure to use it within two months. You can freeze all of them if desired.

Step 15: Preheat the oven to 350°F.

Step 16: Place the pan and ramekin in the oven and bake until golden brown on top.

Step 17: If you think the edges are burning, wrap the edges of the pie pan and ramekins with foil.

Step 18: When you bake the frozen pie, make sure to thaw it for some time before placing it in the oven.

Veggie Loaded Cottage Pie

Makes: 12-15 small pies
Age: 10 months +

Ingredients:
8 tablespoons canola oil
6 cloves garlic, peeled and crushed
8 large carrots, peeled and finely chopped
2 medium white onions, finely chopped
1.8 pounds minced beef
4 red bell peppers, deseeded and chopped
4 large handfuls spinach leaves
6 tablespoons tomato puree
2 medium zucchinis, finely chopped
2 cans (14.5 ounces each) chopped tomatoes
7 ounces mushrooms, finely chopped
2 teaspoons English mustard
Pepper to taste
4 sprigs thyme, finely chopped

For mash:
4 tablespoons butter
3 pounds potatoes, peeled and cubed
Pepper to taste

Directions:
Step 1: Preheat the oven to 350°F.
Step 2: Place potatoes in a pot. Cover with water and place the pot over high heat and cook the potatoes until soft.
Step 3: Meanwhile, place a large pan over medium heat. Add oil and let it heat. When oil is hot, add onions and cook until soft.
Step 4: Stir in garlic and cook for a couple of minutes.
Step 5: Stir in the beef and cook until light brown, breaking the meat as you stir.
Step 6: Stir in the vegetables, tomatoes, tomato puree, vinegar, and mustard and mix well.
Step 7: Cook covered on low heat until the vegetables are tender.
Step 8: Mix in the spinach, thyme, and kale. Add pepper and stir.
Step 9: Uncover and cook until the sauce is thick. Turn off the heat.

To make mashed potatoes:
Drain off the potatoes and add them back into the pot. Add butter and pepper and mash with a potato masher until creamy.

To assemble the pies:
• Take 12-15 small pie pans. (You can use disposable pans if desired.)
• Spoon the meat mixture into the pans. Spread mashed potato on top of the meat mixture. • You can freeze it now. To freeze, make sure to cool completely. Place them on a baking sheet and freeze until firm. Wrap each in cling wrap and freeze until use. Make sure to use it within 3 months. Take out as many pie pans as required and place them on your countertop. Thaw completely.
• Place the pie pans in the oven and bake until golden brown on top and heated through.

Ham and Cheese Muffins

Ingredients:
½ cup whole-wheat flour
¾ cup all-purpose flour
½ teaspoon baking soda
1 teaspoon baking powder
¼ teaspoon kosher salt
1 large egg
10 tablespoons buttermilk
2 tablespoons vegetable oil or canola
½ cup shredded cheddar cheese
1 tablespoon maple syrup
½ cup finely chopped ham

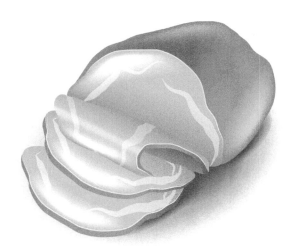

Directions:
Step 1: Preheat the oven to 350°F.

Step 2: Prepare 8-9 muffin cups by greasing with cooking spray.

Step 3: Combine flours, baking powder, baking soda, and salt in a bowl. (Yes, salt is not given to babies but adding salt here enhances the taste of the muffins. You can omit it if desired.)

Step 4: Crack egg into a bowl. Add maple syrup and oil and whisk until well combined. Whisk in buttermilk.

Step 5: Make a well in the center of the flour mixture. Pour the buttermilk mixture into the well.

Step 6: Stir until just incorporated, making sure not to over-mix.

Step 7: Add cheese and ham and fold gently.

Step 8: Divide the batter into the muffin cups, filling up to 2/3 the cups.

Step 9: Bake for 18 minutes or until golden brown on top. Insert a toothpick in the center and take it out. If you see any particles stuck on it, you need to bake for another five minutes.

Step 10: Take them out from the muffin cups and let them cool completely.

Place in a freezer-safe container. Freeze until use. Make sure to use within three months.

To serve: Thaw the required number of muffins and heat for a few seconds in the microwave. You can serve with a little softened butter.

Sweet Frozen
Recipes

Mix N' Match Banana
Ice Cream

Ingredients:
2 ripe bananas, peeled and chopped

For mix n' match fruit flavors use any:
1 cup chopped mango
1 cup blueberries
1 cup chopped strawberries
1 cup raspberries

For mix n' match flavors use any one or more:
2 tablespoons natural peanut butter
2 teaspoons maple syrup
1 teaspoon vanilla bean paste
½ teaspoon ground cinnamon

Directions:
Step 1: Add banana and the mix and match fruit into a Ziploc bag or small freezer-safe container.
Step 2: Freeze until you need it.
Step 3: Take out the bag from the freezer about 10 minutes before blending.
Step 4: Place the banana and fruit in the food processor bowl. (For flavor, you can add any one of the mix n' match flavors. This is optional.)
Step 5: Process until creamy like soft serve.

Notes:
• If you want to use peanut butter, use only banana and no other fruit, but make sure to add maple syrup. It is better to use peanut butter after about eight months of age.

Red Velvet Pancakes with Banana Ice Cream

Ingredients:
2.1 ounces buckwheat flour
½ tablespoons unsweetened cocoa powder
½ egg
½ cup pureed beetroot (roast the beet and puree)
½ teaspoon vanilla extract
1 teaspoon baking powder
½ cup milk of your choice
1 tablespoon melted unsalted butter
1 tablespoon maple syrup
Canola oil to cook

For banana nice cream:
½ can full-fat coconut milk (chilled overnight)
2 bananas, peeled and sliced

For raspberry compote:
2.5 ounces fresh raspberries

Directions:
Step 1: Combine the dry ingredients in a mixing bowl.
Step 2: Whisk together milk, butter, egg, vanilla, and beetroot puree in another bowl.
Step 3: Make a depression in the center of the flour mixture and pour the milk mixture into the depression. Whisk until smooth.
Step 4: Place a large pan over medium heat. Add a little oil into the pan. Swirl the pan to spread the oil. Pour about two heaping tablespoons of the batter into the pan to make one pancake. Make as many as can fit in the pan.

Step 5: Soon bubbles will be visible on top of the pancakes. Cook until the underside is golden brown. Turn the pancakes over and cook the other side as well.

Step 6: Make pancakes until all the batter is done. You can serve the pancakes now.

To freeze:
• Let the pancakes cool to room temperature. Keep the pancakes in a pile, placing parchment paper between the pancakes. You should make three piles.
• Place the piles of pancakes in separate freezer-safe bags (for each pile) and place in the freezer. They can last for about three months.
• A day before serving the pancakes, place banana slices in the freezer and freeze until firm.
• On serving day, make the raspberry compote and banana nice cream.

To make raspberry compote:
• Cook raspberries in a small saucepan over low, mashing with a fork as it cooks.
• Once the raspberries are just warm (not hot), turn off the heat.

To make banana nice cream:
• Take out the can of coconut milk from the refrigerator and remove about a tablespoon of the coconut cream that is floating on top and place in the blender.
• Also add about two tablespoons of the liquid from the can.
• Add the banana and blend until creamy like soft serve.
• Place it in the freeze until you heat up the pancakes.

To serve:
You can heat the pancakes in the toaster or in a microwave before serving.
Spoon some raspberry compote and banana nice cream on top of the pancakes.

Notes:
• To make it vegan, replace butter with oil or vegan butter. Replace milk with non-dairy milk. Omit the egg.

Eggless Pancakes with Pineapple Coulis

Ingredients:

For pancakes:
2 cups plain or buckwheat flour
½ cup whole flaxseeds
Oil to cook
4 teaspoons baking powder
2 cups milk

For coulis on serving day:
½ fresh pineapple, peeled, cored, and chopped
Juice of ½ lemon
½ teaspoon turmeric powder

To serve:
Finely chopped mint leaves
Yogurt
A handful pomegranate seeds (not for babies)

Directions:
Step 1: Combine the dry ingredients in a mixing bowl.
Step 2: Make a depression in the center of the flour mixture and pour the milk into the depression. Whisk until smooth.
Step 3: Place a large pan over medium heat. Add a little oil into the pan. Swirl the pan

to spread the oil. Pour about two heaping tablespoons of the batter into the pan to make one pancake. Make as many as can fit in the pan.

Step 4: Soon bubbles will be visible on top of the pancakes. Cook until the underside is golden brown. Turn the pancakes over and cook the other side as well.

Step 5: Make pancakes until all the batter is gone. You can serve the pancakes now.

To freeze:

• Let the pancakes cool to room temperature.

• Keep the pancakes in a pile, placing parchment paper between the pancakes.

• You should make three piles.

• Place the pile of pancakes in separate freezer-safe bags (for each pile) and place in the freezer. They can last for about three months.

• On serving day prepare the pineapple coulis: Place pineapple, lemon juice, and turmeric in a blender and blend until smoothly pureed.

• You can heat the pancakes in the toaster or in a microwave before serving.

• Top with yogurt and pineapple coulis. Garnish with mint leaves and pomegranate seeds.

Notes:

• You can also freeze the coulis but I am not in favor of it as pineapple may become slightly bitter. It has happened to me a couple of times.

Sweet Potato and Orange Chocolate Truffles

Makes: About 20
Age: 9 months +

Ingredients:
½ cup roasted and pureed sweet potato
3 tablespoons coconut oil
Zest of ¼ orange, grated
2 tablespoons coconut flour
½ tablespoon maple syrup
½ teaspoon orange oil
½ teaspoon vanilla extract or extra orange oil
1 tablespoon cashew butter (optional)
3 medjool dates, pitted
Juice of ¼ orange
1.8 ounces cacao butter
¾ tablespoon cocoa or cacao powder
1 ½ tablespoons tahini

Directions:
Step 1: Place coconut oil, zest, dates, orange juice, and orange oil in a saucepan over medium heat, stirring often.
Step 2: When the mixture begins to boil, lower the heat and cook until the mixture thickens and you may see the oil separating. Turn off the heat and transfer into a bowl.
Step 3: Stir in sweet potato puree until smooth.
Step 4: Add coconut flour and mix until well combined.
Step 5: Freeze the mixture for 20 minutes.
Step 6: Make small balls of the mixture. Insert a toothpick in each. Place them on a plate lined with parchment paper and chill until the cacao butter melts.
Step 7: Place cacao butter, maple syrup, and orange oil or vanilla in a heatproof bowl and place it in a double boiler until the mixture melts. Stir occasionally until the mixture melts.
Step 8: Take out the bowl from the double boiler. Add tahini, cocoa, and cashew butter if using and whisk until smooth.
Step 9: Pick one ball with the help of the toothpick and dip it in the melted chocolate. Place it back on the plate.
Step 10: Repeat with the remaining balls.
Step 11: Remove the toothpicks. Place the plate in the refrigerator. Chill until the chocolate sets.

To freeze: Place the truffles in a freezer bag and freeze until use.

To serve: Take out the bag from the freezer and take out the required number of truffles. Let them thaw completely. You can serve your baby now. For the adults, place truffles in the refrigerator for 15 minutes.

Notes:
• The procedure to roast sweet potato is given in the Lunch chapter (Part 2: Lunch Recipes).

Banana Blueberry Muffins

Ingredients:

1 cup plain all-purpose flour
3 cups whole-wheat flour
2 teaspoons baking soda
3 teaspoons baking powder
1 cup brown sugar
2 eggs
1 1/3 cups mashed ripe banana
2 tablespoons white sugar
2 ½ cups buttermilk
½ cup olive oil
14 ounces frozen blueberries

Directions:

Step 1: Preheat the oven to 350°F.

Step 2: Prepare two muffin pans of 12 counts each by greasing with cooking spray.

Step 3: Combine the dry ingredients in a mixing bowl.

Step 4: Whisk together buttermilk, eggs, oil, and banana in another bowl.

Step 5: Make a depression in the center of the flour mixture and pour the milk mixture into the depression. Whisk until just incorporated, making sure not to over-mix.

Step 6: Add blueberries and fold gently.

Step 7: Divide the batter into the muffin cups, filling up to ¾ the cups.

Step 8: Sprinkle white sugar on top of the batter.

Step 9: Bake for 20-25 minutes or until golden brown on top. Insert a toothpick in the center and take it out. If you see any particles stuck on it, you need to bake for another five minutes.

Step 10: Take them out from the muffin cups and let them cool completely.

Step 11: Place the muffins on a tray and freeze until firm.

Step 12: Place the frozen muffins in a freezer-safe container or freezer bag. Freeze until use. Make sure to use them within three months.

To serve: Thaw the required number of muffins and heat for a few seconds in the microwave. You can serve with a blob of butter if desired.

Vegan Mango and Coconut Muffins

Makes: 24 muffins
Age: 9 months +

Ingredients:

4 cups flour
2 teaspoons baking soda
6 teaspoons baking powder
½ cup desiccated coconut
4 flax eggs (4 tablespoons flaxseed meal mixed with 12 tablespoons lukewarm water)
2 teaspoons vanilla extract
2 tablespoons apple cider vinegar
1 ripe mango, peeled and cubed
4 ounces canola oil
5 cups nondairy milk of your choice
1 ripe mango, peeled, cubed, and pureed

Directions:

Step 1: Preheat the oven to 340°F.
Step 2: Prepare two muffin pans of 12 counts each by greasing with cooking spray.
Step 3: Combine the dry ingredients in a mixing bowl, i.e. baking powder, baking soda, flour, and desiccated coconut.
Step 4: Whisk together milk, (flax) eggs, oil, vanilla, apple cider vinegar, and mango puree in another bowl.
Step 5: Make a depression in the center of the flour mixture and pour the milk mixture into the depression. Whisk until just incorporated, making sure not to over-mix.
Step 6: Add cubed mango and fold gently.
Step 7: Divide the batter into the muffin cups, filling up to ¾ of the cups.
Step 8: Bake for 20-25 minutes or until golden brown on top. To check if the muffins are done, insert a toothpick in the center of a muffin and take it out. If you see any particles stuck on it, you need to bake for another five minutes.
Step 9: Take them out from the muffin cups and let them cool completely.
Step 10: Place the muffins on a tray and freeze until firm.
Step 11: Place in a freezer-safe container or freezer bag. Freeze until use. Make sure to use them within three months.

To serve: Thaw the required number of muffins and heat for a few seconds in the microwave.

Notes:

• Once you make the flax eggs, if using, set them aside for about 15 minutes to gel.

Breakfast Cookies

Makes: 24 cookies
Age: 9 months +

Ingredients:
6 ripe bananas, peeled and chopped
1 cup peanut or cashew butter
½ cup olive oil
4 cups oats
2 teaspoons ground ginger
2 tablespoons vanilla extract
2 teaspoons baking soda
2 teaspoons ground cinnamon
8 tablespoons raspberry chia jam

Directions:
Step 1: Preheat the oven to 320°F.
Step 2: Grease a baking sheet with some cooking spray. (You may need two baking sheets or you can bake them in batches.)
Step 3: Blend together bananas, peanut butter, and oil in a blender and blend until smooth.
Step 4: Pour the blend into a bowl. Add oats, ginger, vanilla, baking soda, and cinnamon and mix until well combined.
Step 5: Scoop out the mixture and drop on the baking sheet in cookie-sized blobs. Make sure to leave a gap between the cookies.
Step 6: Flatten the cookies slightly. Make a dent in the center of each cookie.
Step 7: Place a teaspoon of raspberry chia jam in the well. (You can also place the jam in the cookie just before serving, the choice is yours.)
Step 8: Bake for 12-15 minutes. Watch them over for 12 minutes. Once you think it is just done, turn off the oven.
Step 9: Take out the baking sheet from the oven and let it cool completely.
Step 10: You can serve fresh cookies to your baby.

To freeze:
• Let them cool completely.
• Place the cookies on a tray and freeze until firm.
• Transfer the cookies into a freezer and freeze until use. They last for about three months.
• Take out the required number of cookies from the bag and thaw completely.

Notes:
• You can crush the cookies and add them into a bowl of milk. Let them soak for a few minutes. Serve your baby.

Makes: 20 mini-tarts
Age: 10 months +

Strawberry Tarts

Ingredients:
24.9 ounces oats
4 tablespoons maple syrup
2 bananas, sliced
24 mint leaves, finely chopped
10 ounces butter
14.1 ounces Greek yogurt
16 strawberries, sliced

Directions:
Step 1: Preheat the oven to 350°F.
Step 2: Process the oats in a food processor until finely powdered.
Step 3: Pour butter and maple syrup into the food processor and process until dough is formed. If the mixture is not forming into dough, add a teaspoon or two of water and process again.
Step 4: Make 24 equal portions of the dough and press them into 20 mini-tart pans.
Step 5: Bake the crusts in batches in the oven for 25 minutes or until brown on the edges.
Step 6: Take out the tart pans from the oven and let them cool.
Step 7: Meanwhile, prepare the filling: Mash bananas along with yogurt in a bowl until smooth.
Step 8: Divide the mixture among the tart pans. Place strawberry slices on top.
Step 9: The tarts are ready to serve.

To freeze:
• Place the tarts on a baking sheet and freeze until firm.
• Place the tarts in a freezer-safe container. You can place a sheet of parchment paper over the tarts and place another layer of tarts and freeze until use. They can last for about two months.

To serve: Remove the required tarts from the freezer and place them in the refrigerator for a couple of hours.

Passion Fruit
Mini-Cheesecakes

Ingredients:

For crust:
5 ounces pumpkin seeds
5 ounces sunflower seeds
8.5 ounces oats
8 tablespoons canola oil
2 tablespoons maple syrup
1 tablespoon cacao or cocoa powder

For cheesecake filling and topping:
7 ounces cottage cheese
7 ounces cream cheese
3.4 ounces double cream
6 passion fruits
2 tablespoons maple syrup
24 raspberries

Directions:
Step 1: Preheat the oven to 350°F.
Step 2: Grease two mini-muffin pans of 12 counts each.
Step 3: Place oats, cacao, and seeds in the food processor bowl and blend until crumbly in texture.

Step 4: Pour oil and maple syrup into the food processor through the feeder tube (with the machine running) and process until dough is formed.

Step 5: Place a heaping teaspoon of the dough in each mini-muffin cup and press it into the bottom of each cup. You can use a spoon to do so.

Step 6: Bake for 12 minutes.

Step 7: Take out the muffin pans from the oven and let them cool completely. Take out the crusts from the muffin cups and place on a baking sheet.

Step 8: Place cottage cheese, cream cheese, maple syrup, and double cream in a bowl and beat with an electric hand mixer until stiff peaks are formed.

Step 9: Cut open four of the passion fruits and scoop out the seeds. Add the seeds into the bowl of cream cheese mixture and fold gently.

Step 10: Spoon the mixture into the crusts. Cut each raspberry into two halves and place on the filling.

Step 11: Cut open the remaining two passion fruits and scoop out the seeds. Scatter the seeds on the filling and place them in the freezer.

Step 12: Freeze until firm. Transfer them into a freezer-safe container. You can place parchment paper over a layer of cheesecakes and stack some more cheesecakes.

Step 13: Freeze until use. It can last for three months.

Step 14: Remove from the freezer and thaw in the refrigerator before serving.

Moist Banana Bread with Quinoa

Ingredients:

6-8 medium overripe bananas , mashed (about 1.3 pounds mashed)
8 tablespoons maple or agave syrup
6 ounces vegetable oil
6 ounces almond flour or ground almonds
2 teaspoons ground cinnamon
6 ounces cooked quinoa
4 large eggs
8.5 ounces all-purpose or whole-wheat flour
3 teaspoons baking powder
A pinch fine sea salt

Directions:

Step 1: Preheat the oven to 350°F.
Step 2: Prepare two loaf pans (9 inches each) by greasing with cooking spray. Line the pans with parchment paper as well.
Step 3: Place dry ingredients in a mixing bowl.
Step 4: Crack eggs into a bowl and whisk well.
Step 5: Combine banana, maple syrup, and quinoa in a bowl.
Step 6: Add the beaten eggs into the bowl of banana mixture and whisk until smooth.
Step 7: Make a depression in the center of the flour mixture and pour the banana mixture into the depression.
Step 8: Whisk until just combined, making sure not to over-mix.
Step 9: Divide the batter evenly into the loaf pans.
Step 10: Bake for 60 minutes or until golden brown on top. Insert a toothpick in the center and take it out. If you see any particles stuck on it, you need to bake for another five minutes.
Step 11: If you want to serve right away, serve as much as required and freeze the remaining.

To freeze:

• Place the loaves in freezer bags. You can also cut them into slices and wrap them separately in cling wrap. Place them in freezer bags and freeze until use.
• Use within five months.
• Thaw completely. You can warm it up a bit in the toaster if desired.

Chapter 13

Feeding Schedule

Eat, sleep, poop, repeat. This is probably what your baby's daily schedule looks like. (Along with a little playtime of course!) It is entirely in your hands to determine your baby's schedule. The best way to do this is by creating and maintaining a feeding schedule. Since babies require multiple meals at regular intervals, a schedule comes in handy. Once you have a feeding schedule in place, others in the household can also help take care of this responsibility.

As mentioned, all babies are unique and there are no hard and fast rules about a specific schedule they need to follow. That said, they still need a routine or a structure. When it comes to starting your baby on solid foods, it does not mean they do not need their milk feeds. They will still need their breast milk or formula feeds. Along with this, you can start introducing solid foods. As your baby starts growing, you will need to slowly reduce their milk feeds while increasing solid foods. In fact, from when your baby is 6 months old until 12 months, their intake of solid foods will significantly increase, while you will notice a drastic reduction in their milk consumption.

There is no one-size-fits-all approach to sleeping or feeding schedules, but here are some sample schedules you can try.

Six Months Old

7:00 AM: Milk
10:00 AM: Milk
11:00 AM: Solid food
1:00 PM: Milk
4:00 PM: Milk
7:00 PM: Milk

Seven Months Old

7:00 AM: Milk
8:00 AM: Solid food
10:00 AM: Milk
12:00 PM: Solid Food
1:00 PM: Milk
4:00 PM: Milk
7:00 PM: Milk

Eight to Nine Months Old

7:00 AM: Milk
8:00 AM: Solid food
10-10:30 AM: Small snack
12:30-1:00 PM: Solid food
3:00 PM: Milk
5:30 PM: Solid food
7:00 PM: Milk

10-12 Months Old

7:00 AM: Milk
8:00 AM: Solid food
10:00 AM: Snack
12:00 PM: Solid food
3:00 PM: Snack
6:00 PM: Solid food
7:00 PM: Milk

Notes: In these samples, please include your baby's nighttime milk feeds as well. Also, please don't forget to consult your baby's pediatrician before introducing solid foods and the schedule you are following.

Conclusion

"Sometimes the littlest things take up the most room in your heart."

Winnie the Pooh

We are all unique. Similarly, our babies are unique too. Since no two babies are alike, their experience with baby-led weaning or their response to it will vary too. Chances are, what one baby likes might be disliked by the other. So dear parents, understand that this book is meant to merely guide you along the way. It is a process of trial and error to determine what your baby does and doesn't like.

The concept of baby-led weaning (BLW) is incredibly straightforward. As the name suggests, the baby is the leader in this eating style. In BLW, babies are allowed to start feeding themselves from the very beginning. It is not only an easy way to introduce solids to your little one but offers a variety of benefits, too. Mealtimes will become more exciting, help develop the baby's motor skills, reduce the chances of picky eating, encourage consumption of healthy and wholesome ingredients, and are more affordable.

Use the information given in this book to determine whether your baby is ready for BLW or not. Usually, by the time they are around 6 months old, you can start introducing solids to them. From their eagerness to start putting things in their mouth, to sitting up on their own, look out for these signs.

BLW is easy, but that said, you should be aware of the different types of food that your little one should and shouldn't eat. It is advised that babies under 12 months shouldn't be given honey, cow's milk, raw eggs, nuts, certain cheeses, and so on. By following the detailed food list given in this book along with preparation ideas, BLW will become easier. Don't forget to go through the checklist to get started with BLW. Similarly, use the food reaction chart to keep a track of the foods your baby liked and disliked.

Apart from all of this, don't forget to experiment with all of the different recipes given in this book. Do not hesitate to experiment or change the recipes as per your baby's preferences, provided you do not add any foods explicitly prohibited for babies under 12 months of age. Getting your baby used to eating solid foods is a wonderful process. Seeing your little one get accustomed to eating solid foods and enjoying the food you made will make you feel good.

Now that you are armed with all the information you need, the next step is to get started. Gather all the required supplies to make delicious and nutritious food for your little one. Seeing them feed themselves and enjoying the food they are eating will surely put a smile on your face. What more? By using these recipes, you can rest easy knowing that your child is getting all the nourishment they need. That said, be extra patient, supportive, loving, vigilant, and calm as your little tot learns to feed themselves.

Finally, if you enjoyed reading this book, and the recipes included in it, then I would like to ask you for a small favor. Would you be kind enough to take a few minutes to leave a review for this book? I am sure that other parents out there would want to know about your experience with BLW!

Thank you, and all the best!

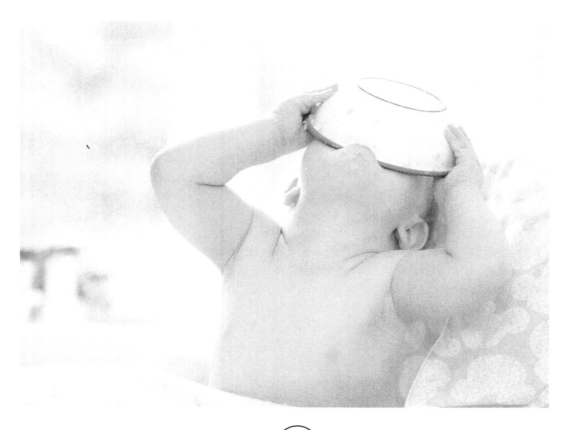

 Thank you so much for purchasing my book.

I know there are many books out there but the fact that you chose mine really means the world to me and it motivates me to carry on doing what I love for me and my children.

So again, THANK YOU! Also, congratulations if you have managed to see all the recipes! I hope you really enjoy making them and feeding your little one.

If I could ask you for one small favor. Could you please consider writing a review on my book? Its literally the fastest and easiest way to support my work as I am an independent author and would really appreciate it.

Your feedback motivates me to continue writing these books which will in turn I hope help you and your little one/ones. It would mean a great deal to me to know how you found the book.

Amazon.com reviews

Amazon.uk reviews

References

10 Amazing Benefits of Baby-Led Weaning (BLW). (2019, August 10). The Postpartum Party. Https://thepostpartumparty.com/reasons-we-loved-baby-led-weaning/

Brown, A., & Lee, M. D. (2013). Early influences on child satiety-responsiveness: the role of weaning style. Pediatric Obesity, 10(1), 57-66. https://doi.org/10.1111/j.2047-6310.2013.00207.x

Cameron, S., Heath, A.-L., & Taylor, R. (2012). How Feasible Is Baby-Led Weaning as an Approach to Infant Feeding? A Review of the Evidence. Nutrients, 4(11), 1575-1609. https://doi.org/10.3390/nu4111575

Cianferoni, A. (2016). Wheat allergy: diagnosis and management. Journal of Asthma and Allergy, 13. https://doi.org/10.2147/jaa.s81550

Clarke, L. (2019, February 21). Baby-Led Weaning Essentials You Need Right Now. Real Parent. Https://www.realparent.co.uk/baby-led-weaning-essentials/

Conte, K. (2021, March 5). 8 Foods You Should Avoid Feeding Your Baby. What to Expect. https://www.whattoexpect.com/first-year/baby-feeding/foods-babies-shouldnt-eat

Emmerik, N. E., de Jong, F., & van Elburg, R. M. (2020). Dietary Intake of Sodium during Infancy and the Cardiovascular Consequences Later in Life: A Scoping Review. Annals of Nutrition & Metabolism, 76(2), 114-121. https://doi.org/10.1159/000507354

Foods to avoid giving babies and young children. (2020, December 7). Nhs.uk. https://www.nhs.uk/conditions/baby/weaning-and-feeding/foods-to-avoid-giving-babies-and-young-children/

Gill, K. (2019, August 28). How Can You Get Your Baby on a Feeding Schedule? Healthline. https://www.healthline.com/health/parenting/baby-feeding-schedule

LaFee, D. (2021, May 10). Best Baby-Led Weaning Equipment for Starting Solids in 2021-Piece of Cake Parenting. Pieceofcakeparenting.com. Https://pieceofcakeparenting.com/best-baby-led-weaning-equipment/#features-blw-plates-bowls

Mercury Levels in Commercial Fish and Shellfish (1990-2012). (2020). FDA. https://www.fda.gov/food/metals-and-your-food/mercury-levels-commercial-fish-and-shellfish-1990-2012

Petre, A. (2019, May 17). Baby-Led Weaning: Benefits, Foods, and Safety. Healthline. Https://www.healthline.com/nutrition/baby-led-weaning#benefits

Rice and Pulses | Agricultural Marketing Service. (n.d.). Www.ams.usda.gov. https://www.ams.usda.gov/grades-standards/rice-pulses

Sachs, M. (2010). Baby-led weaning and current UK recommendations - are they compatible? Maternal & Child Nutrition, 7(1), 1-2. https://doi.org/10.1111/j.1740-8709.2010.00278.x

Taylor, M. (2018, June 28). Baby-Led Weaning | What to Expect. Whattoexpect. https://www.whattoexpect.com/first-year/feeding-baby/baby-led-weaning/

Vincent, R., MacNeill, S. J., Marrs, T., Craven, J., Logan, K., Flohr, C., Lack, G., Radulovic, S., Perkin, M. R., & Ridd, M. J. (2021). Frequency of guideline-defined cow's milk allergy symptoms in infants: Secondary analysis of EAT trial data. Clinical & Experimental Allergy, 52(1), 82-93. https://doi.org/10.1111/cea.14060

AGiAMMy. (n.d.). Toddler eating [Pixabay]. https://pixabay.com/photos/baby-eating-toddler-child-kid-blw-6245143/
Andrade, F. (n.d.). Tofu Nugget [Unsplash.com]. https://unsplash.com/photos/ZimIwyvYeBM

Arze, S. (n.d.). Mini Quiche [Unsplash.com]. https://unsplash.com/photos/oeTdIanecpY
avitalchn. (n.d.). Healthy eating [Pixabay]. https://pixabay.com/photos/child-kids-children-food-eating-1566470/

Baby Weaning. (n.d.). Baby weaning Pixabay. https://pixabay.com/photos/baby-bite-boy-child-cute-eat-84686/

congerdesign. (n.d.). Mixer Smoothie [Pixabay]. https://pixabay.com/photos/mixer-smoothie-mix-healthy-fruit-3709019/

congerdesign. (n.d.). blueberry muffin [Pixabay]. https://pixabay.com/photos/muffins-blueberry-muffins-cakes-3371523/
iha31. (n.d.). Blueberry oatmeal [Pixabay]. https://pixabay.com/photos/blueberries-oats-oatmeal-healthy-531209/

No-longer-here. (n.d.). Baby Must haves [Pixabay]. https://pixabay.com/illustrations/baby-boy-accessories-elements-220296/

Phochiangrak, W. (n.d.). Sweet potato fries [Pixabay]. https://pixabay.com/photos/potatoe-potatoes-potato-sweet-1161819/

RitaE. (n.d.). Banana and Apple Porridge [Pixabay]. https://pixabay.com/photos/cereal-porridge-breakfast-healthy-3186256/

Rita, S. (n.d.). Fruit bowl [Pixabay]. https://pixabay.com/photos/fresh-fruits-bowls-fruit-bowls-2305192/

Redfern, L. (n.d.). Chicken clear soup [Pixabay]. https://pixabay.com/photos/clear-broth-soup-bowl-of-soup-1623462/

safran7. (n.d.). Vegetable pancakes [Pixabay]. https://pixabay.com/photos/food-vegetarian-vegetables-zucchini-3167497/

Staziker, T. (n.d.). Toddler laughing [Pixabay]. https://pixabay.com/photos/child-boy-toddler-music-laughing-1528308/

svibhandik. (n.d.). Green puree [Pixabay]. https://pixabay.com/photos/spinach-soup-green-soup-health-3530522/

Tyson. (n.d.). Family time [Unsplash.com]. https://unsplash.com/photos/hzNavqkrQUA

Wellington, J. (n.d.). colorful popsicles [Pixabay]. https://pixabay.com/photos/popsicles-strawberry-popsicles-red-3571086/

Wurzinger, B. (n.d.). Pumpkin soup [Pixabay]. https://pixabay.com/photos/soup-pumpkin-coconut-pumpkin-soup-1787997/

WyattBing. Acai Berry Bowl - https://pixabay.com/photos/acai-bowl-healthy-breakfast-organic-6607821/

MapleHorizons, Strawberry & Apple Sauce - https://pixabay.com/photos/food-healthy-diet-nutrients-3245379/

KampusProduction, Salmon & Corn Chowder - https://www.pexels.com/photo/a-woman-teaching-a-baby-girl-how-to-eat-7414397/

Irina2521, Smoothie - https://www.shutterstock.com/image-photo/baby-food-homemade-fruit-puree-variety-1733792837

Scrambled egg -Wiktory, https://www.shutterstock.com/image-photo/bowl-creamy-scrambled-eggs-children-75206027

Healthy Mac n cheese -Wiktory, https://www.shutterstock.com/image-photo/mac-cheese-shot-story-on-homemade-132289436

Vegetable Soup -Pamuk, https://www.shutterstock.com/image-photo/childs-food-cream-soup-marrow-potato-136447805

Dinner Prep Picture - Vanessa Loring, https://www.pexels.com/photo/man-carrying-a-baby-beside-a-woman-5082040/

Healthy Pizza -Sedir, https://www.shutterstock.com/image-photo/mini-pizza-114612778

Butternut Squash Soup -Kuvona, https://www.shutterstock.com/image-photo/fun-food-kids-delicious-healthy-pumpkin-1818366017

Baby Bolognese -Lopolo, https://www.shutterstock.com/image-photo/child-girl-eating-spaghetti-lunch-making-1189042480

Banana Muffins -Anna_Pustynnikova, https://www.shutterstock.com/image-photo/healthy-vegan-oat-muffins-apple-banana-409170868

Chicken Pot Pie - Africa Studio, https://www.shutterstock.com/image-photo/tasty-baked-chicken-pot-pie-on-626255318

Cottage Pie -istetiana, https://www.shutterstock.com/image-photo/shepherds-pie-traditional-british-dish-minced-754264087

Blueberry & Avocado Smoothie Bowl - https://www.rawpixel.com/image/3283245/free-photo-image-drink-blueberry-blue-smoothie

Banana & Blueberry Fritters - Aris Setya, https://www.shutterstock.com/image-photo/banana-fritters-pisang-goreng-indonesian-snack-699660343

Baby Eating Cookie - Janine Bronkhorst - https://www.shutterstock.com/image-photo/baby-eating-cookie-630779633

Hash Browns, Nata Bene - https://www.shutterstock.com/image-photo/hashbrown-hash-brown-potatoes-fried-pancakes-1715849323

Mini Pancakes, Kiian Oksana - https://www.shutterstock.com/image-photo/heap-mini-pancakes-on-light-background-1329138110

Breakfast Cookies, Pixel Shot - https://www.shutterstock.com/image-photo/board-tasty-banana-cookies-on-color-2030623886

French Toast Sticks, Rimma Bondarenko - https://www.shutterstock.com/image-photo/healthy-summer-breakfast-baked-french-toasted-1074246947

Cottage Cheese with Fruit, Vladislav Noseek- https://www.shutterstock.com/image-photo/cottage-cheese-curd-fresh-summer-berries-1622095723

Egg & Cheese Muffins, Lilly Trott - https://www.shutterstock.com/image-photo/savory-cheese-bacon-muffins-coffee-on-186786026

Beef Stew, Natalia Lisovskaya – https://www.shutterstock.com/image-photo/beef-meat-stewed-potatoes-carrots-spices-563328664

Pumpkin Risotto, Alexandra Anschiz – https://www.shutterstock.com/image-photo/rice-dish-pumpkin-risotto-on-plate-229034794

Macaroni & Cheese with Broccoli & Cauliflower, nana77777 – https://www.shutterstock.com/image-photo/gratin-85171354

Pea Fritters, OnlyZoia – https://www.shutterstock.com/image-photo/fried-vegetable-patties-on-plate-delicious-543826816

Broccoli Soup, Africa Studio – https://www.shutterstock.com/image-photo/composition-bowl-creamy-baby-vegetable-soup-741036961

Chicken & Pea Carbonara, Kiian Oksana – https://www.shutterstock.com/image-photo/homemade-pasta-green-peas-chicken-cream-293974094

Kale Pesto Chicken Quesadilla, mama_mia – https://www.shutterstock.com/image-photo/stack-mexican-quesadilla-chicken-corn-sweet-439452439

banana chia seed pudding, Natashamam – https://www.shutterstock.com/image-photo/healthy-diet-breakfast-overnight-oatmeal-chia-1022197933

fish cakes, A. Zhuravleva – https://www.shutterstock.com/image-photo/fried-fish-cakes-on-white-plate-1564163869

Vegetable Pancakes, Elena Shashkina – https://www.shutterstock.com/image-photo/zucchini-pancakes-herbs-108012467

Meatless Meatballs, Alexander Raths – https://www.shutterstock.com/image-photo/fried-meatballs-parsley-leaf-isolated-on-1944895012

Chocolate potato truffles, Rika777 – https://www.shutterstock.com/image-photo/vegan-truffle-chocolate-potato-cake-on-1946900926

Banana Bread, A_Lein – https://www.shutterstock.com/image-photo/healthy-banana-bread-cake-breakfast-1562825053

Soup, Ahanov Michael – https://www.shutterstock.com/image-photo/pumpkin-baby-soup-puree-wooden-backgroung-494057446

Quinao & peas, Liliya Kandrashevich – https://www.shutterstock.com/image-photo/quinoa-salad-green-pea-mint-on-401895625

Pea Risotto, Lapina Maria – https://www.shutterstock.com/image-photo/italian-risotto-rice-green-peas-mint-157256036

sweetcorn soup, Amarita – https://www.shutterstock.com/image-photo/corn-soup-bowl-319598321chi

Chicken Soup, PJjaruwan – https://www.shutterstock.com/image-photo/bowl-chicken-broth-isolated-on-white-478596541

Chickpea Couscous, Martin Rettenberger – https://www.shutterstock.com/image-photo/tabbouleh-made-couscous-various-vegetables-152563280#

Brown rice pudding, stephanie frey https://www.shutterstock.com/image-photo/delicious-sweet-pumpkin-custard-rice-brown-37916431

Tofu nuggets, Mark Marcos – https://www.shutterstock.com/image-photo/tofu-nuggets-mayo-dip-2106840002

Spaghetti Bolognese, Oksana Kuzmina – https://www.shutterstock.com/image-photo/adorable-oneyear-baby-toddler-try-catch-1066806974

Baby equipment, Africa Studio – https://www.shutterstock.com/image-photo/bright-baby-tableware-bib-on-yellow-508386595

Baby with food, Onjira Leibe – https://www.shutterstock.com/image-photo/top-view-little-boy-holding-food-1621728304

Baby Eating, Jack Photographer – https://www.shutterstock.com/image-photo/baby-eating-by-hand-omelet-vegetable-1285567873

Baby finished plate, Alexandr Grant – https://www.shutterstock.com/image-photo/kid-plays-kitchen-dishes-645931519

Father feeding baby, Monkey Business Images – https://www.shutterstock.com/image-photo/father-feeding-baby-daughter-high-chair-627677921